# IDEAS AND THE
# UNIVERSITY
# LIBRARY

Recent Titles in
**Contributions in Librarianship and Information Science**
SERIES EDITOR: Paul Wasserman

# IDEAS AND THE UNIVERSITY LIBRARY

## ESSAYS OF AN UNORTHODOX ACADEMIC LIBRARIAN

Eli M. Oboler _____

*Contributions in Librarianship and Information Science, Number 20*

GREENWOOD PRESS
WESTPORT, CONNECTICUT · LONDON, ENGLAND

**Library of Congress Cataloging in Publication Data**

Oboler, Eli M
 Ideas and the university library.

 (Contributions in librarianship and information science ; 20)
 Includes indexes.
  1. Libraries, University and college—United States—Addresses, essays, lectures.
 2. Libraries—United States—Addresses, essays, lectures. I. Title. II. Series.
 Z675.U502            027.773                      77-11
 ISBN 0-8371-9531-4

Library of Congress Catalog Card Number: 77-11
ISBN: 0-8371-9531-4
ISSN: 0084-9243

First published in 1977

Greenwood Press, Inc.
51 Riverside Avenue, Westport, Connecticut 06880

Printed in the United States of America

# ACKNOWLEDGMENTS

The articles, talks, letters, verse, and other writings which appear
in this book are reprinted with approvals and copyright acknowledg-
ments as indicated below. I am grateful to all the original publishers
for their permission to reprint.

"What Is a Librarian?" reprinted from *Library School Review* (Octo-
 ber, 1968), pp. 9-11.
"The Scholarly Library," first printed as "Invitation" in *Idaho Li-
 brarian* (April, 1955), pp. 37-41.
"Ideas and the State University," first printed in *School and Society*
 (February 4, 1967), pp. 78-80; also printed in Stanley Lehrer, ed.,

*Leaders, Teachers, and Learning in Academe* (New York: Appleton-Century-Crofts, 1970), pp. 143-47.

"Machines and Libraries," from *Iconoclast* (Summer, 1966), pp. 7-13.

"Good-bye, Reference Librarians," from *RQ* (September, 1964), pp. 12-13.

"The Irrelevance of Relevance" reprinted by permission from the April 1970 issue of the *Wilson Library Bulletin*. Copyright © 1970 by the H. W. Wilson Company.

"Browsing at ISC Library," from *Idaho Librarian* (July, 1955), pp. 49-50.

"Faculty-Library Cooperation," from *Improving College and University Teaching* (Spring, 1956), pp. 38-43.

"Get-'em-All Theory" is a combination of a letter in *Library Journal* (March 15, 1960), p. 1046, and an article in *Library Journal* (October 1, 1960), pp. 3391-92.

"Cooperation Among Idaho's Academic Libraries" appeared in the *Bookmark* (Moscow, Idaho) (September, 1970), pp. 7-8.

"Selling the Academic Library" was printed in: Allan Angoff, ed., *Public Relations for Libraries*, pp. 133-49. In somewhat modified form, a portion was printed as "Displays for the Academic Library," *Idaho Librarian* (October, 1970), pp. 135-38.

"Copy Rights and Wrongs," from *Idaho Librarian* (April, 1969), pp. 63-69.

"O. P. and All That," from *ALA Bulletin* (October, 1953), pp. 433-34.

"Sights, Sounds, and Print," from *Idaho Librarian* (July, 1973), pp. 95-99.

"The Library Patron's Bill of Rights," from *Idaho Librarian*, pp. 59-62.

"Library Associations," from *Drexel Library Quarterly*, 3, no. 3 (July, 1967), pp. 255-62.

"Intellectual Freedom, Censorship, and Library Associations," from *Drexel Library Quarterly*, 3, no. 4 (October, 1967), pp. 399-400.

"What the Individual Means to ALA," from *ALA Bulletin* (February, 1961), p. 185.

"A Constitutional Crisis in the ALA?" from *ALA Bulletin* (April, 1966), pp. 384-86.

"Attitudes on Segregation," from *Library Journal* (December 15, 1961), pp. 4233-39.

"The Case for ALA Regional Annual Conferences," from *ALA Bulletin* (September, 1969), pp. 1099-1101.

"Library Statistics," from *Idaho Librarian* (January, 1962), pp. 6-8.

"The Accuracy of Federal Academic Library Statistics" reprinted by permission of the American Library Association, from *College & Research Libraries* (November, 1964), pp. 494-96.

"Academic Library Statistics Revisited" reprinted by permission of the American Library Association, from *College & Research Libraries* (November, 1967), pp. 407-10.

"Hallelujah, Give Us a Hand-Out, and Revive Us Again!" from *Idaho Librarian* (April, 1966), pp. 46-48.

Letters to the Editor:

"Research and Reality" reprinted by permission of the American Library Association, from *College & Research Libraries* (March, 1960), pp. 184-85.

"A Brief Rejoinder to Bateson," from *Journal of General Education*, 14 (April, 1962), pp. 69-71.

"Misquoted, Misunderstood, and Reduced to Absurdity," from *Library Journal* (November 15, 1960), pp. 4076, 4078.

"Re: Library Research," from *Wilson Library Bulletin* (September, 1967), p. 23.

"Court Ruling . . .," from *Chronicle of Higher Education* (May 1, 1972), p. 6.

"Basting the 'Livers With,' " from *American Libraries* (December, 1971), p. 1144.

"Faculty Status for Librarians" reprinted by permission of the American Library Association, from *College & Research Libraries* (January, 1973), pp. 69-70.

Verse:

"The Pace of Reading," from *Essential Books* (February, 1956), p. 36. © 1956 by Essential Books, Inc. Reprinted by permission of Oxford University Press, Inc.

"Sabbatical Leave," from *AAUP Bulletin*, 57, no. 31 (September, 1971), p. 376.

"Accreditation Visit," from *Journal of Academic Librarianship* (November, 1975), p. 9.

Oboler Dicta:

Most never printed before, except no. 38 (*Library Journal,* February 15, 1967, p. 742); no. 33 (*Library Journal,* March 15, 1967, p. 1131); no. 4 (*Library Journal,* May 1, 1967, p. 1798); and no. 36 (*Library Journal,* June 1, 1967, p. 2124).

*For My Father and Mother*

# CONTENTS

# PREFACE

The chapters which follow were written originally not as parts of a book but as articles in various magazines, or they were given as talks to library associations. They do have, it is hoped, a certain unity as statements of fact and opinion reflecting the professional life of an academic librarian in America in the generation between the post-World-War-II euphoria of the early 1950s and the bicentennial frenzies of post-Watergate 1976. No updating, reflecting a 20-20 hindsight, has been practiced.

In the increasingly complex world of communications, the academic librarian will continue to be highly placed in the information hierarchy.

Academic librarianship is, and should be, as much an art as a profession—and reading the material which is printed in this volume may just possibly serve both a teaching function for the tyro and a stimulating or, at best, an inspirational one for the active practitioner. Being an academic librarian is, as one of the chapters herein suggests, both a privilege and a responsibility, and, fortunately, on many occasions and for many of us, it is fun.

*Pocatello, Idaho*                                                                                      E.M.O.
*Idaho State University*
*July, 1976*

# IDEAS AND THE UNIVERSITY LIBRARY

# 1 DEFINITION

## WHAT IS A LIBRARIAN? OR MOUSETRAPS, BEEHIVES, AND SHARK ANKLETS

The modern librarian is a . . . no; librarianship today includes in-for . . . that won't work either. Let's try *Through the Looking Glass.*

Remember the White Knight? Yes, the one who went forth to battle so very well equipped. To his saddle, you will recall, was fastened "a very good beehive, one of the best kind. But not a single bee has come near it yet. The other thing is a mouse-trap." Why a mousetrap on a horse's back? . . . "if they *do* come, I don't choose to have them running all about." The White Knight felt, "It's as well to be provided for *everything.*"

And that is what the librarian of today seems more and more to be—a White Knight on a charger, caparisoned cap-a-pie with the raiment of information retrieval, the mousetrap of operations manage-ment, and a "very good beehive," filled with no bees. Sometimes one wonders why today's students of librarianship bother to go to library school anyway. Surely the College of Business Administration would be the better spot.

It is, after all, the physicists and mathematicians and engineers who can probably best train you to understand and use efficiently the computerized library that is just around the corner, and has been for some years now. No one can better train the systems analyst, the budgeteer, the gray-flannel-suited, pipe-smoking business executive type, than the business administration professor.

Out of some form of McLuhanalysis will surely come the best preparation for librarians in a world where, we are constantly being reminded, "the medium is the message." Or even "the massage"! Here the psychiatrist, the expert in linguistics, the media expert will all come into play. As philosopher Abraham Kaplan tells us:

the intellectual foundation of library science . . . can be provided by nothing other than the whole set of disciplines which I lump together

under the name of "metasciences." These are sciences not about
subject matters provided by man and nature, but our idea *about* man
and nature, or by our language, or by our ways of transmitting and
processing the information we have derived, and so on.

What Kaplan meant by this, he further explained, was "disciplines
like mathematics, logic, linguistics, semantics, and, in the narrower
sense, theory of information, and maybe cybernetics. These disciplines then range off into other related metasciences." At least he
was good enough to tell us that the reason for this "centrality" of
these metasciences is "not because they underlie the new computer
technology or related technologies like miniaturization, but for an
intellectual reason, because there is central to them the concept of
structure, of order, of form, which seems to me to be precisely the central concern also of library science."[1]

And there we have it, if we agree with the good doctor. Simply
spend your academic years at this important group of matters, and
you are going to be the best kind of intellectual librarian.

Now, whether or not you can combine this kind of a background
with the business training suggested earlier and also with, to give Dr.
Kaplan credit, what he calls the "humanistic basis" of library education, which "includes not only a certain appropriate set of beliefs
about what men are like and what they are up to, and how they
make use of ideas, but also a certain appropriate set of values," is
another question.

Stop! Surely we are back to the White Knight again. Remember
that the Looking Glass World's White Knight had anklets placed
around the feet of his horse. Why? "To guard against the bites of
sharks." "It's an invention of my own," said the Knight.

Put on your own anklets. The sharks in the library education and
experience field are many and clever; they'll bite, unless your anklets
are firmly attached.

Actually, you don't need *any* training in real librarianship in these
days to be a good librarian. When Alice told the Knight, who kept
falling off his horse, "I'm afraid you've not had much practice in
riding," the Knight asked, a little offended at the remark, "what
makes you say that?" Alice replied, "Because people don't fall off
quite so often, when they've had much of practice!" The Knight

could only answer, very crossly, "I've had plenty of practice ... plenty of practice."

The White Knight's "new way of getting over a gate" is somewhat
reminiscent of some of our recent, more unusual approaches to
getting simple, routine library tasks done. You'll recall the Knight's
approach: "first I put my hand on the top of the gate—then the
head's high enough—then I stand on my head—then the feet are high
enough, you see—then I'm over, you see." Alice reasonably enough
remonstrated, "Yes, I suppose you'd be over when that was
done.... but don't you think it would be rather hard?" You will all
recall that the White Knight (like all too many of our *Luftmenschen*
in librarianship) had to say, "I haven't tried it yet ... so I can't tell
for certain—but I'm afraid it *would* be a little hard," which made him
"vexed."

So off you go into the bright new world of the mechanized and
metascienced library with your beehives, and your mousetraps, and
your anklets of all description. If you never meet a shark, if you
never see a mouse, if you never catch a bee, surely you are all
prepared to take care of whatever sharks, mice, and bees come along.

May I be serious, to conclude this, and suggest that actually there
are some examples and exemplars that may be of even more value to
you than the White Knight or the more rarefied atmospheres of
philosophy. Just possibly you could do worse than spend your library
education years (which include your entire life, if you hadn't realized
it) in somehow aiming toward acquiring the discriminating bookish-
ness of a Larry Powell or a William Carlson, the analytical precision
of a Dewey, a Dana, or a Ranganathan, a Cutter or a Lubetzky, the
pedagogical concern of a Shera or a Rothstein, a Wilson or a
Carnovsky, the broad national and international view of a Clapp or a
Putnam, a Panizzi or a Francis, the willingness and ability to define
and redefine the ever-changing dimensions of intellectual freedom
evinced by an Asheim or a Gaines, a Merritt or a Fiske, the easy
familiarity with the groves of academe shown by a Metcalf or a
Tauber, a Vosper or a Lundy, the empathy with the young of a
Henne or a Spain, a Darling or an Edwards, the urban and urbane
awareness of a John Richards or a Lowell Martin, of a Hamill or a
Greenaway, or even the socially conscious brashness of a Josey or a
Cushman, a Levy, or (putting it very immodestly) an Oboler. Putting

all these together wouldn't necessarily come close to producing The Librarian, but would certainly produce a *librarian*, and not an educational media specialist or a systems analyst or a media coordinator!

The librarian of tomorrow, like the librarian of today and the librarian of yesterday, must be of his times, but must also partake of the traditions of his profession. These traditions may seem anachronistic and, mayhap, even useless. But they deserve examination to see just why they have endured for at least discussion purposes until now.

The tradition-bound librarian we will always have with us. The librarian who can see the value of nothing that has not been suggested today, or at least no more lately than the day before today, is also always around. But the librarian who will improve his profession is the one that reconciles the two extreme points of view and faces up to his fundamental obligation, which has not changed since the days of that "Babylonian named Amil-anu, who lived in the reign of Emug-sin, king of Babylonia" almost 4,000 years ago, or of "Nabu-zuqub-gina, who had charge of the collection from the sixth year of Sargon, 716 B.C., to the twenty-second year of Sennacherib, 684 B.C."[2]

Then and now, the major responsibility of the librarian was to be "keeper of the books." Everything beyond that, really, comes under the heading of mousetraps, beehives, and shark-avoiding anklets.

Look behind the rhetoric and the semantic confusion of the purported prophets of librarianship who are so confusing us today, and, fundamentally, you will find that a librarian is a librarian, and so may it always be. We are all debtors to our profession, and it richly deserves our spending a professional lifetime in paying that debt in unalloyed, nonbrummagem coins of the bibliothecal realm.

## THE SCHOLARLY LIBRARY

Imagine yourself in Egypt in the days of the early dynasties. It is fifteen years before the end of the first dynasty, or 3200 B.C. The highest of priests, the priest of Seshait, is conducting an important public function. He is "stretching the cord" for a new temple, a building which he has planned. "Stretching the cord," or laying out the ground plan, corresponds to our ceremony of "laying the cornerstone." The priest of Seshait is not only priest but also architect and, of all professions, librarian for King Senedi. The goddess, Seshait, of course, was the wife of the god Thoth and is expressly called "She who draws in her horns, mistress of writings, mistress of buildings, the lady of libraries." Her husband—the moon god of Egypt, Hermes to the Greeks, and Mercury to the Romans—is referred to as "Lord of the hall of books."

Magic played a very great part in Egyptian life. Since knowledge of what was maintained in the writings on papyruses gave super-human power, books were necessarily kept from the common people. During the time of Ramses III, in the twelfth century B.C. a famous conspiracy headed by the queen took place. One of the major charges in the trial which followed the exposure of the plot was that two librarians, or scribes of the archives, had unlawfully permitted the conspirators to have a so-called magic roll. For this crime, these librarians were put to death. As you can see, it is not without some precedent that traditionally librarians have been reluctant to make public their precious possessions, the books.

The first truly modern library, that of Ptolemy II, the museum library of Alexandria, flourished in the third century B.C. According to the historian Josephus, Demetrius Phalerius, library keeper to the king, finally had a separate library building, although the library previously had been part of the king's palace. Now, having the new building, he

was endeavoring, if it were possible, to gather together all the books that were in the habitable earth, and buying whatsoever was any-where valuable, or agreeable to the king's inclination (who was very earnestly set on the collecting of books); to which inclination of his Demetrius was zealously subservient. And when once Ptolemy asked him how many ten thousands of books he had collected he replied, that he had already about twenty times ten thousand, but that, in a little time, he should have fifty times ten thousand.[3]

This first recorded reference to a librarian and an administrator harmoniously working together to build up a library collection is certainly worthy of note. The extent to which this cooperation went is just possibly a little beyond what might be expected in modern times. For instance, Ptolemy confiscated all the books found in any ships which happened to anchor in the harbor of Alexandria. Indeed, the librarian went so far as to borrow from Athens the original texts of the works of Aeschylus, Sophocles, and Euripedes. When pressed for the return of these books, he returned not the original text which had been borrowed but only a transcribed copy which he had made.

The first library of which we are aware which is somewhat like our modern college and university libraries is the library in the Athenian Academy, located within the Ptolemeum. Here, for the first time, not only officials and those directly involved in scholarship were permitted the use of the manuscripts, but also all educated men were permitted access. In fact, according to Vitruvius, this library was *ad communem delectationem*, "for the enjoyment of all." The Romans built up vast libraries by bringing home Greek books along with other captured items, and perhaps a description of a Roman library might be appropriate:

so far as stonework, architectural style, and artistic decoration are concerned, libraries resembled the other monumental structures of the age. Very likely there was always a statue of some deity which was placed usually in a recess of the great hall. Accompanying it were busts and medallions of scholars and writers "whose immortal souls speak in these very places" (*immortales animae in locisiisdem loguuntur*). A good deal of ornamentation was in evidence, but in order to spare the eyes, gold was avoided and a greenish marble selected for the floors. The book rolls, with tickets bearing their titles outward, lay in the pigeon-holes of the wooden presses. These were often symmetrically arranged and sunk into niches in the walls. When necessary, there were several such rows, one above the other. The top rows were then reached by means of galleries, which rested on columns.[4]

During the later Roman Empire, librarians were regularly attached to the court. According to a letter from Theonas, bishop of Alexandria (282-300 A.D.) to Lucianus, a chamberlain of Diocletian at his palace in Nicomedia:

The chief chamberlain ought, therefore, to know all the books which the emperor possesses; he should often turn them over and arrange them neatly in their proper order by catalogue; if, however, he shall have to get new books, or to have old ones transcribed, he should be careful to obtain the most accurate copyists; and if that cannot be done he should appoint learned men for the work of correction, and recompense them justly for their labors. He should also cause all manuscripts to be restored according to their need, and should embellish them, not so much with mere superstitious extravagance as with useful adornment; and, therefore, he should not aim at having all the manuscripts written on purple skins and in letters of gold unless the emperor has specially commanded that. With the utmost submission, however, he should do everything that is agreeable to Caesar. As he is able, he should, with all modesty, suggest to the emperor that he should read, or hear read, those books which suit his rank and honor, and minister to good use rather than pleasure. He should himself be thoroughly familiar with those books, and he should often commend them to the presence of the emperor, and set forth in an appropriate fashion the testimony and the weight of those who approve them, in order that he may not seem to lean upon his own understanding only.[5]

During the Middle Ages book stocks were very meager. Since there were so few manuscripts, and since what additional ones there were were mainly the result of years and years of painstaking copy work, it was natural that the monks kept very close watch over their precious belongings. In addition to providing the manuscripts with ownership marks, so-called book-curses were inscribed on them to frighten away any prospective thieves. Strict regulations concerning the procedure for lending books have been found in the rules of some monastic orders. We are told that "on an appointed day in the year the brothers assembled in the chapter house. There those who had borrowed books the last time were called by name and required to return them. Then the business of lending books for the next year proceeded. All this was under the direction of the *librarius,* who also had to keep lists of the books lent."[6] For any lent outside, both a receipt and a deposit were required.

By the twelfth century, monasteries generally had entirely forbidden anyone besides their own members to borrow books. Perhaps the first true college library was the library of the Sorbonne, founded about 1250 by Robert de Sorbonne, Louis IX's chaplain. His will left the college named after him his own library, which soon became the outstanding library of the whole University of Paris. Fellows of the college were provided with keys, with other members of the university being allowed to use the books under strict rules, and with strangers requiring an introduction from some scholar. The most frequently used codices were chained to their desks. Those which were duplicates or seldom used material were loaned on condition that a pledge was left, usually consisting of another book of equal value.

With the Renaissance and the discovery of printing, libraries began to be opened up. Instead of keeping books chained on desks, books were placed in rows in book cases which ran along the walls. As the pressure of new additions made it necessary to extend cases all the way to the ceiling, galleries were built to permit easier access to the upper shelves. Sir Thomas Bodley came to Oxford to restore the university library, which had been destroyed some time before. According to his rules the Bodleian Library was to be open five hours each day, but only graduate students were given free access to the shelves. The British Museum, opened in London in 1759, had rules providing "free access to all studious and curious persons." Actually, many formal rules barred the library to most. As we can see from its name, the British Museum was intended to be more for exhibit purposes than as a place for study.

Most influential of German librarians was Gottfried Wilhelm Liebniz. We are told that

> he measured the value of a library not by the number but by the quality of its books. . . . Small, "curieuse" volumes he thought more important than thick tomes with contents devoid of sense. The heaviest emphasis he laid on regular acquisition of continuations and new books: neglect of this practice would involve the decline of the entire collection. A necessary presupposition for all this, however, was the availability of an adequate yearly appropriation.[7]

An outstanding German library, based on Liebniz's principles, was that of Gottingen University. Its first curator, the somewhat interestingly named Baron von Munchhausen, worked to build up this library. He "took personal charge of buying books, arranged to be represented at all important auctions, and kept up a steady business with foreign and domestic book dealers. Consideration was always given to wishes of the professors," says the chronicler.[8] Professor Gesner, who was actually the library director, in one of his reports laid down the requirement, which bears repetition, "that the librarian not, like a financier, merely accumulate capital consisting of books, but must share his wealth with as many as possible."[9]

By the end of the eighteenth century the Gottingen Library was by far the most outstanding in Europe. It was even said, to quote the historian, "that the proud Gottingen professors owed their scholarly success solely to the university library."[10]

During the early nineteenth century the growing German universities all suffered from a particular malady. On this subject I again quote from Alfred Hessel's *History of Libraries*. "The all powerful library committee was a disastrous creation for it led mostly to the already meager funds being ear-marked for the use of individual professors."[11]

Robert von Mohl, librarian at Tübingen in 1836, announced "the chief librarian, whatever else he may be, must think and plan night and day for his library; in its behalf he must buy and exchange, beg, and—one might almost add—steal." Despite this strong statement, he too was unsuccessful in eliminating the library committee's influence.

Next among great librarians to affect library methods and architecture was Sir Anthony Panizzi, who in 1856 became principal librarian of the British Museum. In addition to permitting all to use the books, he also made many changes in the old hall-with-gallery type of building. His plans involved separate rooms for readers and shelving books.

This all too rapid and sketchy selection from library history as it concerns the scholarly library cannot hope to give any detailed study of the great libraries of our day. The building which we are dedicating today is based on the most modern principles, but without forgetting some of the useful and fundamental classical ideas cited in this brief statement.

College libraries have only comparatively recently begun to give the kind of service that they should have given always to their patrons. An eastern university recently celebrated a notable anniversary of its longevity; as part of that celebration, a multivolume history was published which includes this reference to how one part of that university functioned in the 1870s:

Some measure of the nature of the College may be inferred from the quality of its library, which might well have seemed inadequate even to a man who took no more than an ordinary pleasure in reading, but which must have been a nightmare to a scholar, for the librarian allowed books to be drawn for no more than an hour and a half daily, and . . . "he generally seemed displeased when anyone asked for a book and positively forbidding when asked to buy one."[12]

This is *definitely* not a library in *that* tradition.

Some years ago Isaiah Bowman, then president of the Johns Hopkins University, gave an address at a meeting of the "Friends of the Library" at Johns Hopkins. He said:

A library is not merely a collection of books but a Hall of Records of human experience and thought, where one may retrace, step by step, the path along which striving man has toiled. Like the great books on their shelves, libraries contribute an immortal quality to civilization. . . . Were it not for a combination of industry, interest, and devotion on the part of those who build and those who work in libraries, we should in many instances not have, and in many more instances not have available, the choicest human records that still bring inspiration, knowledge, and guidance to the souls of men.[13]

It is, of course, in the spirit of such men as Bowman, Liebniz, and Demetrius Phalerius that I offer to the students, the faculty, and the administration of Idaho State College, indeed, to *all* interested in reading and everything that it signifies to our state and our country, a heartfelt, sincere invitation to make use of this library and its contents. This is a library planned both to preserve reading materials and to permit them to be used easily and efficiently. Without readers any library is but a vast mausoleum; with you, the words in the books come alive and once more are part of the great active heritage of Western culture.

One thing should be stressed in that invitation, namely, that it is not just a rhetorical statement. Any resident of the state of Idaho, and for that matter, any person who really has need of them, is welcome to use our facilities. Naturally, we are first and foremost a library for the college community; but the community outside the campus is more than welcome to make use of what we have to offer, subject to the first demands of our students and faculty. We are open seven days and four nights a week, eleven months in the year, and we hope to see all of you and be of service to you in the days and years to come.

## NOTES

1. Abraham Kaplan, "The Age of the Symbol—A Philosophy of Library Education," in ed. Don R. Swanson, *The Intellectual Foundations of Library Education* (Chicago: University of Chicago Press, 1964), pp. 13-14.

2. James Westfall Thompson, *Ancient Libraries* (Hamden, Conn.: Archon Books, 1962), p. 12.

3. Ernest Cushing Richardson, *Biblical Libraries* (Princeton: Princeton University Press, 1914), p. 162.

4. Alfred Hessel, *A History of Libraries* (Washington, D.C.: Scarecrow Press, 1950), p. 26.

5. Moses Hadas, *Ancilla to Classical Reading* (New York: Columbia University Press, 1954), pp. 26-27.

6. Hessel, *A History of Libraries*, p. 26.

7. Ibid., p. 72.

8. Ibid., p. 74.

9. Ibid.

10. Ibid., p. 75.

11. Ibid., pp. 81-82.

12. *A History of Columbia College on Morningside* (New York: Columbia University Press, 1954), p. 16.

13. Isaiah Bowman, *A Design for Scholarship* (Baltimore: Johns Hopkins Press, 1936), pp. 56-58.

# 2 CLARIFICATION

## IDEAS AND THE STATE UNIVERSITY

Matthew Arnold once described Oxford as the "home of lost causes, and forsaken beliefs, and unpopular names, and impossible loyalties." This description could well be used for every responsible and worthwhile university in the United States today. If a university is not the "home of lost causes, and forsaken beliefs, and unpopular names, and impossible loyalties," what is it?

The university, particularly the state university, today all too often is the home of the causes that have already been won, of beliefs that are held by everyone else, of faculty and administrators who strive only to be popular, and of those who have perfectly ordinary and conformist loyalties. Indeed, for many state universities, the question of the relationship of ideas and the university hardly comes up. The state university today is much too busy with taking care of the workaday problems that it must face, what with inadequate space, too few faculty, too few library books, and an ever-growing student body, to have any time to think of such outré things as "ideas."

Most of our state universities have some kind of slogan which indicates that they are trying their best to be "the servant of the state" or, as some universities have put it, "the state is our campus." If this slogan is carried through to its logical potentialities, it means the destruction, rather than the regeneration, of the university.

That university which strives to put as its primary function that of being a service agency to a government, whether local or state or federal, is, by that very action, abnegating its most important role, which is to be the creator and disseminator of new and updated ideas. Very rarely, indeed, do political entities countenance new ideas. Their function is to maintain the status quo and to protect that which is, rather than to look into that which may be, and even, possibly, to try their best to circumvent the possibility that what now is may develop into some kind of ineluctable necessity of what must be.

14

Sacrifices to political or other nonuniversity-related exigencies affect, to a greater or lesser extent, just about every university in the country. Even without going into panic about the possibility of "socialism" in the ever-increasing role of the federal government in almost every phase of American civilization, it is still possible to be concerned, if one cares about the facilitation of free inquiry, with the dire potentialities of the current trend toward centralization of control of research and even teaching. For example, in the tremendous library at Moscow University, which numerically is perhaps the largest in the world, certain books are denied to students. Some other books may be given out only with the approval of the powers that be. Every piece of reading material that is charged out must be signed for, and this record is maintained for each student or faculty member, to show what he has read throughout his years at the institution. This is not quite the way in which the records of libraries in American state university libraries are kept.

Getting down to specifics on the campus community's responsibility toward freedom of inquiry, the faculty of a university has a very heavy responsibility, which transcends meeting classes, advising students, or even that most vital of all duties, participation in faculty committee meetings. The basic responsibility of the faculty of a university is to encourage and to disseminate ideas of past time, our time, and of time to come. Nowhere else in our society can this obligation be placed. Nowhere else is there such a comparatively free group of individuals, with the sound educational background and with the time and opportunity to do the job that needs to be done.

But what is happening to the faculty's basic job? Just as one example, according to a *New York Times* article of August 1, 1965, written by the education editor, Fred M. Hechinger, "The nation's universities are entering a new phase as they respond to a growing demand that higher education become the agent of urban service and renewal." There is still one more job for the university and its faculty. There are voices to the contrary, however. The president of the American Council on Education, Logan Wilson, has urged educators, to remember that "our primary obligation to students in residence implies a top priority for the teaching function."

This gets into rather a complex question, namely, one of priority. What good is having ideas and communicating just to students in residence? On this basis, it would take a long, long time for the fermentation of ideas of universities to reach the general public. Even today, just five and a half million of our population are attending academic institutions at any one time. The obligation to get ideas out from the cloistered, ivy-covered walls is as important as the one of having the ideas in the first place.

These ideas must be, by their very nature, destructive, iconoclastic, new ideas. The majority of the population is always against destroying the old and must always be reassured that whatever suggestions there are about the new will not be of a revolutionary character. All ideas, to some, are dangerous; but to suppress ideas is much more likely to be dangerous.

There is a new phrase which has come to signify the so-called new trend in our universities, that of community involvement. It is only a new phrase, not really a new idea, however. The University of Wisconsin has said repeatedly that "the boundaries of the campus are the boundaries of the state." It becomes more and more apparent that the university of the future must have as its boundaries the world. This sounds very idealistic. But when have new ideas coming from a campus not sounded idealistic?

We are all too closely tied together under that sword of Damocles of which the late President Kennedy warned us—the constant threat of nuclear destruction—to have any delusions about being able to be as parochial as the state-as-boundary motto would make us. Perhaps it is a necessary motto, for the sake of getting backing from provincially minded legislators, to help in getting basic budgets. Perhaps, in order to get nationally based grants, this may, at this time, have to stop at being some such slogan as "the boundaries of the campus are the boundaries of the United States." The importation of ferment-stirring new students into practically every institution of any consequence in the country, the exportation of professors by such means as Fulbright grants, and the new idea (at least new for most of the many institutions which now have it) of sending students away for intervals of from one to several years into institutions of learning throughout the world, are examples that tie in with the notion that ideas are universal rather than parochial.

What is the place of the student body in this idea of the relationship between ideas and the university? Our generation of students is quite different from the so-called quiet generation, of which some of us complained, back in the 1950s. In the 1960s, it is being a conformist to be a protester, to be an activist, to cry out against silence, apathy, privatism, and to be actively involved in national problems. The student "explosion" at Berkeley has been only the outward sign of feelings that are present in almost every institution of higher learning these days. It is not only proper to picket and march these days; it is almost de rigueur.

The average college student today is faced with quite a dilemma. He normally comes to an academic institution for the purpose of learning. He does not see himself in the role of a crusader or a picketer or as the leader of a revolt. He is simply going to spend four years in learning those things which he needs to learn in order to fit into our society. This is a fair description of the wants of the majority of students at a majority of American universities. But, of course, there is a very active minority which sees the university as a place to do as well as to learn.

What should be the role of ideas in a university, both for students and for faculty—and, perhaps most importantly of all, for the administration? Ideas should be central in the university, for all three groups mentioned. The sacred fact is but a tool, and the sacred idol of an established opinion or a generally accepted idea is, except to the confirmed believer in the sacredness of that which is, again but an instrument.

Nobody wants irresponsibility in the university. It is not a gathering place for the crackpots of the world. It should be a place where those who have something to think about, who are able to express their thoughts clearly and understandably, who have responsible and measured facts and opinions underpinning their beliefs may express those beliefs, whether or not it pleases a legislature or a pressure group or even the president of a university.

The university, ideally speaking, must treasure the individual who brings new ideas as its true leader. That individual, whether instructor or full professor, whether a freshman or a graduate student, whether a white Anglo-Saxon Protestant or a brown Buddhist or a member of the Jewish faith, may have something to add to the ideas which are the only justification for the university's existence.

It is true that there are very clear indications, if public opinion polls are to be believed, that the general public is not necessarily in agreement with what has been offered hereinbefore as the ideal. According to what pollster Louis Harris found out from what he calls "a carefully drawn cross-section of the adult public," the American public is not very tolerant of nonconformity. To quote him, "the man who stands apart from the crowd—because he does not believe in God, because he pickets against the war in Vietnam, because he demonstrates for civil rights—is regarded as harmful to the American way of life by two out of three of his fellow citizens."

Here is the way the question was asked: "America has many different types of people in it but we'd like to know whether you think each of these different types of people is more helpful or more harmful to American life, or don't they help or harm things much in one way or the other?" When asked about college professors active in unpopular causes, 58 percent of this cross section of the American public considered this kind of behavior more harmful than helpful to American life. Only 6 percent considered it helpful, and 36 percent said it did not matter. It is rather disturbing to find that college professors active in unpopular causes were ranked as more harmful to American life than members of the John Birch Society, who received a vote as follows: 48 percent said they considered them more harmful than helpful, 4 percent more helpful than harmful, and 48 percent said they did not matter to American life as far as helping or harming is concerned. This may all be irrelevant, because universities can hardly be run on the basis of public opinion polls. What is more significant than what people think of the thinking individual is what happens to his thought, which ultimately is the more important in deciding what action takes place.

The ideas which truly matter are those which change the world. The ideas which keep the world as it is are of some importance, but only until the newer ideas come along which will make the older ideas obsolete. Out of the university, the American university in particular, have come many, if not most, of the ideas which have created the civilization we have today. If this civilization is to be improved—and certainly in every aspect of life a need for improvement is evident—most of the ideas for the improvement, perhaps even for the preservation of the very structure of that civilization, will come out of the university.

So long as the university is willing to hire and keep the men who have the unconventional ideas, to keep in school the students who question the conventional wisdom, and to make public proudly and freely those ideas which do come from the university, rather than to pretend that somehow these controversial ideas have nothing to do with the university as such, the American university may be proud of itself. Once it begins to go down the road of denying in any way the opportunity for ideas, the university, as such, is dead.

## THE VECTORS OF TOLERANCE

Several thousand years ago, Aristophanes described the situation in the Greek civilization of his time like this: "Whirl is King, having driven out Zeus." Now, in our American civilization—if "civilization" *is* the correct description of what we have—of 1976, just about the same situation exists.[1]

We *have* no leaders, we *have* no true Establishment, we *have*, seemingly, no sense of history. Whirl *is* definitely king. The title of this article deals with that whirl, that turbulence. I am certainly no mathematician, but I *am* a lexicomaniac of sorts. The word *vector*, so often misused these days, is a *very* useful word in speaking and discussing some of the pressures on librarians today. In a strict, mathematical, dictionary sense, vector is "a complex entity representative of a directed magnitude, as of a force or velocity." A vector *field* is presently defined as "a set of vectors defined at the various parts of a curve or a region of space." In the wildly agitated and agitating field of communications of ideas and facts and opinions and feelings, the librarian—public or school or academic—is being battered about, whether he or she realizes it or not, by a multitude of vectors.

Now, as to *tolerance,* that, too, is a term which is not always clearly understood. In the mathematical or technological sense, it is used as "a specified allowance for error in weighing or measuring, or for variation from the standard or given." It is now generally used as the "disposition to . . . allow the distance of beliefs, practices, or habits from one's own." One dictionary says that tolerance requires an attitude of forbearance (especially intellectual forbearance in regard to those activities or opinions or views with which one's self is not fully in sympathy).

Most appropriate of all, in my opinion, is the definition of tolerance used in medicine; that is, "constitutional or acquired capacity to endure shock, a poison, or, especially, a food or drug which may be harmful if taken in excess," as well as the power of resistance to such. Tolerance originally meant, but is now rarely used for, "the act or posture of, or the capacity for, bearing suffering or hardship."

A leading current authority on the topic, Glenn Tinder, however, stresses the importance of returning to the etymological origins of the word to discover what he calls "fundamental nature."[2] He sees tolerance as best defined as "bearing, or suffering, the conditions imposed by others." Among the conditions to which he refers as "other-intruded" are these: "estrangement, uncertainty, historical insecurity, and a divided mind (divided between love and the allowance of distance, understanding and doubt, trust and suspicion)." This group of conditions of intolerance are those, says Tinder, which "keep one from enjoying self-sufficient, secure, and personal existence." All that is quite an argument in favor of maintaining the highest possible degree of social tolerance. It is an obligation, in Tinder's terms, which accepts "the rights of others to express themselves in all of their disturbing reality."[3]

Now, let me return to consideration of some of the vectors which are now affecting or will affect the intellectual and academic freedoms of libraries. First, it is pretty hard to deny that *basically* American civilization—particularly in the upper Northeast, the Midwest, and the South (and, let me quickly add, in my own region—throughout the Rocky Mountain states as well)—is basically a white, Anglo-Saxon, Protestant civilization. And not just Protestant, but *Calvinist,* Fundamentalist Protestant—Neo-Puritan Protestant. The concomitants of Puritanism—the urge to censor, the desire to control, the hypocrisy of acting one way and talking another—all are present in the new drive for the denial of intellectual freedom.

As just one example, witness the efforts in the last few years throughout the country to act as though Darwin and his fellow evolutionists never existed. California has, since 1969, had an altered biology curriculum in its public schools which states that "the Book of Genesis presents a reasonable explanation of the origin of life and . . . the concept of special creation should be taught as an alternative to the concept of organic evolution." It is almost as if the

Scopes trial of 1925 never took place! Despite some $7 million spent by the National Science Foundation in the 1960s to create so-called modern biology courses in the important schools of America, there are a great many states (not just California) which have textbook controversies mainly reflecting the same hidebound points of view which have fought the teaching of the theory of evolution. Dorothy Nelkin,[4] in the April, 1976, issue of the *Scientific American*, documents "The Science-Textbook Controversies," in an article by that name, and sees the nationwide picture as basically a difference of opinion between those who believe in the complete authority of science and those who don't. Oddly enough, it is just possible that the people who protested against the MACOS series of books in Kanawha County, West Virginia, in 1975 and the antievolutionists throughout the country are more representative of true intellectual freedom beliefs than the one-valued and single-minded "liberals" who oppose them. But this kind of grass-roots opposition in the public schools is bound to have its reflections in the public libraries and the academic institutions as well . . . probably sooner than we think.

To carry this a little further, it is probably not exactly a secret to any academic group that, nationwide, higher education is not at its peak of public acceptance. Decided drops in new-student growth, the renamed "vocationalism" (now misnamed "career" education), the overabundance of college graduates in terms of nationwide demands for such—put these and some more education-restricting situations together, and the declining budgets in our academic libraries should be no surprise. Curiously, we know we have over 10 percent of our population who are functionally illiterate, but this undereducation seems to bother Americans far less than the claimed overeducation already described.

Americans in general have always had a slightly suspicious, questioning, and doubtful view of the intellectual, the thinker for thinking's sake. In today's terms, the man who thinks for a living lacks *machismo*.

A couple of years ago a national study was made to ascertain *who* the American intellectuals were. Suffice it to say that these objectively chosen intellectuals were *not* among the people best known to the average American. They were certainly not the ones who appear on the "Johnny Carson Show" or on the front pages of the newspapers or even on the covers of the popular news magazines. A great many more Americans will listen to and identify with Muhammad Ali or Fred Lynn or Rick Barry than with Robert Nisbet or Irving Kristol or Nathan Glazer. And the record of intellectuals in American politics—the Adlai Stevensons, the Woodrow Wilsons, the Eugene McCarthys—is not too impressive. Indeed, most politicians will tell you it is a greater handicap than a benefit to be considered a "thinker," not a "doer," by the electorate. So these are just a few of the vectors impinging on the kind of tolerance I am sure we would like to have evidenced in our libraries.

Or *would* we?

I am well aware of the conventional wisdom about academic librarians, that we are the crème de la crème, the elite of librarians, especially as relates to intellectual freedom. Yes, we know about the Fiske and Busha studies, but surely *we* aren't guilty of such manifest contradictions as pasting the Library Bill of Rights on the door of a locked room where we hide away "controversial" books. No—of course not! Or do we violate the Library Bill of Rights? Well, let me pose a few questions to which you may have your own answers. For instance, should you ever *not* purchase a particular book, even when funds are available, because Professor Blank, Head of Department X, differed with the opinions in that book? In other words, does your intellectual freedom extend only as far as the power of a faculty member will let it? No, I am sure that such an occurrence or any situation like it *never* happened to you!

Or for another instance, have you ever refused to subscribe to *Playboy* or the *Berkeley Barb* or the *Village Voice* for a supposedly "good" reason (which *you* know, deep in your professional conscience, is only a rationalization prompted by fear of consequences of one sort or another)?

Or, still another example, when local movie-house operators have dared to show a couple of X-rated movies in a row and get picketed by the local "concerned citizens" group, did you say even a *single* public word in remonstrance?

Now, where are we? We are talking about the pressures on the right to be different and to express one's self differently. Almost by definition, the librarian must be tolerant—able to take that shock referred to in the medical definition, to allow for error as in the mathematical definition, and, finally on this matter of definition of the word *tolerance,* to have a solidly based disposition to allow into his or her library *other* beliefs and practices and habits from his or her own. This is not really an easy assignment.

Research into the personality profiles of the so-called tolerant personality reveals some interesting things. Contrary to what one might think, tolerant persons are not always particularly lucky in interpersonal relations; exceptionally tolerant individuals seem more likely to be tolerant of groups, generally, than of other individuals. The tolerant person is inclined to be, in summary, "rational, humanistic, liberal in social attitudes." He or she would seem to be more inclined to wit and humor than to be a sobersides. Perhaps the single most characteristic attitude of the individual who is tolerant, according to Professor James Martin of Wayne State University, is that he has an "attitude of 'fair play' . . . a refusal to hate people who could be hated with impunity."[5]

Martin's research further indicates that tolerant persons are usually more likely to be found among younger people than older ones, of at least lower middle-class status, with more than average education, in urban rather than rural areas, and *not* reared in an authoritarian family environment. On this whole point, Martin summarizes by saying that "the composite tolerant person might be illustrated by a young, white Unitarian minister from a Northern urban community," who will probably vote "for a Catholic-Negro Southerner for president." Why? Because of "common political attitudes."

What we must all be aware of is that each in his own library is fighting one of a number of battles that add up to a war—a war against ignorance, a war against anti-intellectualism, indeed, a war against the freedom to choose not only the kind of books there should be in a particular library but also the right to choose one's way of life. Perhaps this point can be most vividly illustrated by telling you about Aleksandr Nikitenko. This man served for over fifty years, between 1826 and 1877, in various capacities in different offices of the Censorship Department of the Ministry of Education of the Imperial Russia of the Czars, in St. Petersburg, Russia. His major function was to keep the Russian people from reading anything which might disturb the status quo, the Establishment, the rulers of Czarist Russia. What if the work submitted for judgment was written by men now regarded as the great writers not only in their time but perhaps *all* time—authors of the stature of Turgenev, Gogol, Pushkin, Balzac, Scott, and Dumas. No matter; the censor was there with his little scissors or defacing pencil.

Russia, under the Czars, had a most elaborate system of censorship, including separate secular, military, and ecclesiastical censors. In fact, at one time during the 1850s there were no less than twelve different groups involved in censorship. These included:

a general one in the Ministry of Education, a Chief Censorship Administration, a 'supreme secret' committee, an ecclesiastical section, a military section, a censorship section in the Ministry of Foreign Affairs, a theatrical one in the Ministry of the Imperial Court, a newspaper section in the Post Office Department, a censorship unit in the Third Section of His Majesty's Private Chancery . . . now a new one—the pedagogical . . . [and] a section for works on jurisprudence in the Second Section of His Majesty's Private Chancery, and there is the foreign book section.

One must give Nikitenko credit for this much; he was self-critical enough to know (and deplore) some of the results of the work of the censor, at least in his earlier years. As he wrote in his diary (published in a very readable translation by the University of Massachusetts Press under the title of *The Diary of a Russian Censor*),[6] "why worry about acquiring knowledge in school when our mode of life and our society stand in opposition to all great ideas and truths, when any attempt to realize any sort of idea related to justice, good, or the public welfare, is branded and persecuted by you as a crime?" There are a great many things about this book that sound exactly like what we in the United States sometimes seem to be getting into. In 1843, the Russian Minister of Education, to whom the Central Censorship Committee reported, said that he wanted to see an end to all Russian literature. Then, he said, "at least we would know where things stand," and "I shall sleep peacefully." And certainly that is something we all should worry about, whether the censor sleeps peacefully or not!

In 1844, a pseudonymously authored volume entitled *Deception in the Caucasus* caused an official uproar, after being passed by the Moscow censor (Nikitenko was in St. Petersburg). When the Russian

Minister of War read this particular book, he was "horrified" to read it, because, he said, "this book is particularly dangerous because there is truth in every single line of it." I hardly think any comment is necessary.

Read Nikitenko, and then reread the many official and unofficial accounts about CIA and FBI activity through the last twenty years or so. You shouldn't have to be exhorted to become involved with your state association's intellectual freedom committee and with the Intellectual Freedom Round Table, to have a personal and a library subscription to the *Newsletter of Intellectual Freedom*, and particularly to have in your library and understanding ALA's *Intellectual Freedom Manual*, which I think is a guide that would be of very great practical benefit to any librarian, academic or not.

Speaking of the *Intellectual Freedom Manual*, it includes one particular section which I especially recommend for the professional reading of the academic librarian. The section on "Academic Libraries and Intellectual Freedom" highlights some illustrations of the fact that, despite the generally accepted opinion—to which I referred earlier—academic librarians (among various types of librarians) are the least likely ones to be guilty of internal censorship practices, there are some things with which academic librarians should be concerned. Here are just a few:[7]

1. There should be a written down, specific statement of procedure, familiar to appropriate members of the library staff, as to how to handle those requests from students for particular titles or better coverage of specified subject areas, which are all too often neglected. All of us certainly do our best to work with faculty in trying to build up the library collection, but do we give students their fair voice in this significant intellectual enterprise?
2. There is hardly a library in existence which does not have some kind of "restricted access" area, but be sure that you don't use your locked room or rare book room or locked case simply as an easy way to hide away the items which might develop into some kind of controversy, or might otherwise be troublesome.
3. *No* book should be marked in the card catalog, whether by a star or special letter or in any other way, to single it out as a "dangerous" book, or for any reason except to protect it from

likely thievery or vandalism. And with modern methods of book guarding, even this seems highly suspect as a justification for such book labeling.

4. Be absolutely sure that your circulation policies are really not inequitable or likely to give inadequate time for reasonable use of materials to any particular group of users.

5. We all are aware that the current national code for interlibrary loans, since it does not give equal service to undergraduates, is clearly not in line with the Library Bill of Rights. No one denies that there are quite strong arguments for this, but expediency is not really a final argument in an issue of this sort. It needs to be resolved soon, if we are to be consistent in our claim to equity and justice in our libraries.

6. All fees which are charged for services, all fines charged for overdues, should be identical for faculty and students. There is no reason for faculty members having any special "breaks" simply because they are members of the faculty.

And that is just a preliminary list. It could be made a great deal longer if you just walk through your library. Try to *think* intellectual freedom rather than "this is the way we have always done this." You'll be surprised how many changes you can suggest in long-standing (but not, therefore, automatically permanently justified) rules and procedures which in trivial ways, or quite significantly, negate intellectual freedom and violate tolerance.

Finally, let's look at the big picture. If a "fever" chart of American tolerance were being kept, it is obvious the 1960s and 1970s would not rank very high. Watergate and all it stands for (or perhaps, all we, the American people, stood for!) and the Vietnam war and related phenomena in our own country were not exactly conducive to toleration. A marked change in our social mores, what has been called the sexual revolution, clearly has had its repercussions in our books and films and other materials which are available for library purchase and distribution. It is hardly possible, as we all know, to buy a novel from any major publishing house which is free of so-called four-letter words or of scenes which would be rated at least "PG" in any movie house.

The more or less prevalent Puritanism, so characteristic of our nation through the three and one-half centuries since the landing on Plymouth Rock, is not likely to vanish in the foreseeable future. It could very well be that a new wave of anti-intellectualism, also demonstrably characteristic of our country, is on its way. There are many indications of this trend, but most important of all, there is also a strong American tradition in the line of freedom, most significantly for us in the terms of this discussion, in the line of *intellectual* freedom.

Just as one among a myriad of possible examples of Founding Fathers' beliefs, James Madison, in a private letter he wrote in 1822, said, speaking of colleges, that "learned institutions ought to be favored objects with every free people, they throw that light over the public mind which is the best security against crafty and dangerous encroachments of the public liberty."[8] Remember that, you who are academic librarians; you have high and great responsibilities. Don't stand in the way of that right about which Madison was concerned. Rather, be sure you help out in dealing with the problem which Madison described in the same letter, "a popular Government, with all popular information, with the means of acquiring it, is but a *prologue* to a farce or tragedy; or, perhaps, both." "Knowledge," he further wrote, "will forever govern ignorance; the people who mean to be their *own* governors must arm themselves with the power which knowledge gives."

I have been a practicing academic librarian for a full generation now; it was 1946 when the late Ralph Beal thought I might make a possible librarian for the University of Chicago's Harper Memorial Library's Reserved Book Room. I've seen great fads and frills in academic librarianship come and go since then. Once the movie film was going to replace the codex book completely; then microforms would miniaturize everything; then television would close up all the libraries. Today we are engulfed in nodes and paths, minicomputers, and a million other gadgets and notions. One thing, I fervently hope, will never change—our mutual resolve to live our lives for intellectual freedom rather than to let our profession die by censorship, external or self-imposed.

We must always remember that without intellectual freedom, freely and openly and actually in practice, not just given lip service, we are only book *distributors*. With it, we can say and prove we are *librarians,* worthy of the 200-year heritage of independence which began in Philadelphia's Independence Hall and that 100-year heritage also begun in Philadelphia by Melvil Dewey and his compatriots.

We who are privileged to share in the proud and inspiring profession of librarianship will, for we must, face the vectors of tolerance with courage, with determination, and with that knowledge which will, in the long run, overcome our greatest enemy, ignorance.

## MACHINES AND LIBRARIES:
## THE PARAMETERS OF COMMON SENSE

The above title immediately will give some of you the notion that there is a deliberate dichotomy of the machine and the library and perhaps even that the intent of the writer is to present machines as nonsensical and libraries as by nature imbued with common sense.

Not at all ... never underestimate the importance of a bit of punctuation. Please note the colon which separates the title from the subtitle. Actually, this article, if we were still using the eighteenth-century mode of self-description in a work's subtitle, would probably bear some such long-winded supplementary appellation as "The Adventures of a Traditional and Troubled Librarian Amidst the Confusions and Contradictions of the Over-Inflated Claims of Some of the Documentalists and Information Retrieval Specialists and the Closed Minds of Most of the Rest of Us."

I have nothing against the machine. I hope it goes without saying that I have nothing against the library. But combining the more outré machines with the library has not always, in my unsophisticated opinion, brought about results commensurate with either the effort necessary or the relative value of the old way.

There is an unfortunate tendency on the part of some tradition-bound librarians to attempt to ignore the machine and its current or even potential effect on the library. Their head-in-the-sand attitude is reminiscent of Thomas Carlyle's famous comment on the statement by Margaret Fuller, "I accept the Universe." The doughty old Scot, you will recall, said, "Gad! She'd better!' "

But accepting the machine as a fact of modern library life does not mean we must swallow all the overexaggerated claims and fantasy hopes associated with the computer and its fellow robots as Gospel. As Ira Gershwin said, "Oh, I take the Gospel, whenever it's pos'ble, but with a grain of salt!"

Enough of generalizations. Let me quickly state my thesis. This is that the librarian of today, be he reference librarian, cataloger, circulation head, administrator, or the lowest man on the library totem pole, should know what the current limits are in his own library in terms of staffing, space, available budget, and practicality. His motto should not be, if I may paraphrase a statement well known to all, "Ask not what the machine can do for you; ask what you can do for the machine."

It is of this latter attitude which I would speak. Lately, to judge from some talks I have heard at library conferences and from articles that I've read in recent library literature, the attitudes of most who write and speak about the subject has seemed to be about as hopeless as those of the Babylonian mothers sacrificing their young to the molten jaws of Moloch and Baal. The machine has just about taken over, in some libraries, regardless of true need or even of reasonable cost.

Let us take one example. A strong trend, in the past few years, has become evident toward the making of book catalogs. To take the word of some devotees of this technique, all that is needed to solve the majority of our library problems is to start key punching, and out will come strong magic to do our work. To be a mite facetious, the very holes seem to be holy!

But let us face some somber facts à la the Carlyle-Fuller exchange, cited earlier. A very recent study, written by Paul Wasserman, dean of the newly established Graduate Library School at the University of Maryland, lists the following as "dangers" to the library which decides to mechanize. First, as Wasserman points out, computer time is not always as available after a while as at first. As he says, "the research prestige and academic influence of other departments may succeed in elbowing the library aside."[9] Also, Wasserman stresses, routines for machine systems are quite costly to develop, and, once determined, cannot be changed without considerable difficulty."[10] He reminds us that mechanization brings, as he says, "rigidity of operating procedure which tends to reduce the area of human latitude, sharply curtailing the exercise of staff judgments on exceptions and variations, and in the ability of clients of the system to effect variations from the usual processing routines."[11]

Wasserman is quite eloquent about what is probably the most difficult to answer objection to the mechanization of libraries. He reminds us that social science research has revealed that large organizations with a record of stability, such as is usually the case in library staffs, "tend to be staffed by individuals with lower tolerance for accepting radical change than those in organizations . . . with lesser security of employment." Furthermore, "mechanization advances the acceleration of the formalization of the organization, . . . leading to a reduction in the number of status posts and higher degree of centralized administration."[12]

One danger which Wasserman discusses is well known to most of us, perhaps as more of a reality than a threat. He says, "there is a powerful disposition in organizations to provide more adequate financial support with which to pay for the glamour of novel machinery than for the less glamourous human beings who are also an essential ingredient in the implementation and carrying out of machine procedures."[13]

Of these and other problems attendant to library mechanization, Wasserman sees as "the greatest problem . . . the need to carefully and clearly assess exactly what it is which the process seeks to accomplish, than to reassess each component task in order to ascertain whether or not it leads logically and efficiently to this end." He states, and I agree entirely with this, "a machine is in no way a substitute for the human mind in identifying values or the rationality of procedures, for it cannot aid in the choice of alternatives nor can it discriminate except according to a prearranged set of rules which human minds evolve for it to follow."[14]

Wasserman is not unique in his objections. So doughty an authority as Ralph R. Shaw—famed for his invention of the very first practical machine usable for circulation records, as well as for multitudinous studies in the field of mechanizing of library routines—has written, as recently as in the February 1, 1965, issue of *Library Journal,* of "the increasing enthusiasm for things that are different." He also refers to the "almost universal" practice, particularly in the mechanization area, of "publication of aspirations as achievements." As proof of this latter, he cites the National Library of Medicine's

Medlars project, which he states, unequivocally, "is still far from operational" and about which he states "nobody knows whether it will work at all, let alone work more efficiently than other systems."[15]

On the other side, we are given a very good parameter for defining the limits of usefulness of a machine in the library—this time, specifically in a university library. Donald P. Hammer, serials librarian at Purdue, tells us that "the use of machines to accomplish the work of the university library will be limited to clerical tasks. . . ." He states that "a useful criterion to judge the intellectual quality or professionalism of a position will be its lack of adaptability to automation."[16] Here is a brand-new idea, amidst the plethora of repeated and adapted shibboleths about the machine.

Let us look at the Hammer theorem in a rather different light. Granting its validity, then it must follow that anything which adapts easily (whatever that means) to automation requires a low intellectual quality from a nonprofessional. What kind of tasks does Hammer offer as suitable for the machine to handle? His list begins with the preparation of book catalogs which have "a complete record of every item in the library's collection . . . stored in such a way that immediate inquiry and response is possible." This alone somewhat staggers the imagination, but let us go on into the Hammer wonderland.

Next, the computer in the academic library of the future would handle all serials questions—from orders to check-ins to distribution lists to serials catalogs to notices of availability to special lists to statistical analyses and to preparation for the bindery. Gifts and exchanges, acquisitions, cataloging, circulation, reserve book room operation, technical reports collection, budgets and accounting, other library office routines, and even reference work—all fall under this redoubtable Hammer.

But a clear look at the article's terminology may, to use Shaw's wording in his previously cited article, separate "form from substance." In the first place, no library today uses the so-called on-line system with "one or more remote input-output consoles in the library on-line with the computer elsewhere." Hammer admits such a system is "far beyond any now in library use," but states, without giving proof, that "this system is a practical one and not 'the world of tomorrow' type of thing."

He does mention a few "bugs" in the way of various of his proposals. For instance, he admits that at Purdue, the "author catalog contains a few more than 400,000 cards" and that "it has been established that it will require twenty man-years of keypunching to convert it to a computer catalog." Putting this into dollar terms, assuming a working year of about 2,000 hours, and paying two dollars per hour to each key-punch clerk, and having twenty clerks work for one year, the cost would be $80,000 for labor alone. Now this would be just for the author cards, let alone the usual title, subject, and cross-reference cards. Incidentally, the figures for 1963-64 show that the total amount paid out in wages for clerks at Purdue University Library was just $83,660.[17] I would not like to be the person who would try to convince the administration of Purdue University to more than double its clerical costs just to get part of a computer catalog on key punch cards. I can just imagine the reaction when the top administrator is told that the total cost would be in the neighborhood of $400,000 just to get the thing started. Surely this is one of our common sense parameters, namely, fantastic costs.

As I said before, there are times when we who are librarians seem to be on the verge of becoming slaves of the machine. Long ago Ralph Waldo Emerson said, "Things are in the saddle and ride mankind." This is a danger that, of course, cannot be ignored in discussing relationship of the machine and libraries or the machine and the librarian.

Not long ago, a report was made on "Experience in Man and Machine Relationships in Library Mechanization," concerning what happened at the Douglas Aircraft Company Missile and Space Systems Engineering Library between 1959 and 1962, when a mechanized information system was designed to handle technical reports, both their own and those from other sources. Machines used were an IBM 7090 and an IBM 1401, with a Frieden Flexiwriter to take care of input.

According to Gretchen Koriagin, the engineering librarian for Douglas Aircraft Missile and Space Systems, "problems may occur in cataloging personnel or Flexiwriter operators who resist adjustment to the restrictions of the machine. Adjustment results from understanding of the system and corrective motivation. With proper training, a vital interest in the system and an acceptance of the challenge of

mechanization are established." Miss Koriagin continues, "the relia-
bility and value of the system is responsible to the library and the
people providing the library input. The programming is done once
and then 'the bug' will function effectively." And she says, most
revealingly, "the human variations must be minimized through training, motivation, and understanding of the system."[18] If this isn't
suiting the man to the machine, then I don't know what is. I wonder
if it is possible ever to get away from "human variations"!

The parameters of common sense, so far as mechanizing libraries is
concerned, have, to some enthusiasts, had no limits. The head of the
Council on Library Resources, Verner W. Clapp, not long ago inti-
mated that rather than stopping with the usual basic job of librarians—to locate books on a particular topic, or even to go further and
find articles, or even still further to find topics under discussion—"may it not be possible that a word index is what is really
needed?" He said that he admits that "it will probably never become
economically feasible, even though every year that passes makes it a
little less nonfeasible. It would be interesting to speculate on how
such an index might be used if it were available." Of course, we
would have to have indexes of the indexes to words, and in turn
indexes of those indexes. This way lies, if not madness, surely utter
lack of common sense. Clapp makes one particularly useful observation in this article, in stating that "we shall require continuous and
extensive research in the semantics of information processing, in
man-machine interaction, and the development of machines."[19] I
believe that all of this research is in its very beginnings and that we
are a long way from knowing what we are doing and why we are
doing it, particularly as relates to "man-machine interaction." This is
probably the real horizon for those who are concerned with the
future of the machine in the library, but so far, at least, it has
seemed to have the least attention paid to it by the machine minded.

It does not seem to be generally known that an attempt has been
made toward describing the so-called ultimate system for information
retrieval. Several years ago, at a meeting of the Washington Chapter
of the Association of Computing Machinery, a gentleman named
Simon M. Newman presented a paper on the topic "Information
Retrieval: Toward an Ultimate System," and suggested the following
as the approach toward this so-called ultimate IR system. In the first

place, there would be a machine which can "both 'read' and 'understand' documents, i.e., some automatic means to reduce the document to a machine-readable form, some program which can respond to program languages." He says that it is just a matter of time before such a machine will be developed. In fact, he goes so far as to say, "the new system, incorporating both a sophisticated programming and hardware design on the knowledge of languages, should yield the prototype of the ultimate IR system within the next few years."[20]

According to Newman:

when this ultimate system is in operation, the questioner will phrase his question in his normal language and present it to the system. The program for processing the question may then interrogate the questioner on ambiguities it finds in the question, and on the scope and generality of the question. When decisions have been made on these points, and proper wording of the question has been properly settled, the program will direct the revised question to the proper level in the cascade, and facsimiles of the relevant documents will be presented to him.

He admits that, "of course, this preliminary interchange between the questioner and the system may result in the questioner proposing a plurality of questions. The search strategy of the system will decide whether it will be searched simultaneously or serially." He further admits that "such a system will be costly to build, maintain and operate; and it could well be that only one, or at most a few would be created for universal use."

He says as a beginning, "its file could well combine the Patent Office files, those of the Science and Technology Division of the Library of Congress; publications of the Offices of Technical Services, the Atomic Energy Commission, and the National Aeronautics and Space Administration: as well as such quasi-private collections as John Crerar Library and Engineering Societies Library." To make it truly universal, he suggests that "mechanical translation programs could be incorporated in the system, so that documents and questions in languages other than English could be processed. Ultimately, a system might well be placed under the custody and control of UNESCO, or some other international agency."

For Newman, "existing small systems seem adequate for the

limited collections and those of low-frequency use." I agree 100 percent. I also would like to point out that his so-called ultimate information retrieval is really only for science and technology and is, thus, obviously far from the ultimate.

It is interesting to note that some twenty-six years ago when the American Library Association tried to look into "The Library and Tomorrow," very few even came close to suggesting that by 1965 we might be on the way to some kind of mechanized replacement for the traditional library. Frederick P. Keppel, president of the Carnegie Corporation of New York, did see the backstage tasks of the librarian performed by people "tending machines which apparently performed these and other functions at the turn of a dial." Indeed, he says, "in fact, librarianship would seem . . . to be largely a setting of dials. There would be no pages, but instead dial controlled containers would be running all the errands of the library—a little reminiscent of the electrically directed torpedoes of old."[21] This is hardly up to the dreams of today.

In the Encyclopaedia Britannica Book of the Year of 1958, we were told that the home of tomorrow would be a "communicenter." According to the description by Maurice B. Mitchell, president of Encyclopaedia Britannica Films, Inc.:

the library in the communicenter home of tomorrow might very well consist of millions of books. As the great public libraries begin to put their collections on microfilm, people with electronic library cards will be able to view them on their television screens and home microfilm readers. A master library directory in the home will direct them to the "dial number" of any book in the local library, and dialing the number will produce the volume, page by page, on the home microfilm reader. For those whose tastes range beyond the limitations of local collections, long distance calls will be made on the great libraries around the world. The problems of providing space for books in libraries and the deterioration of the books through use and age will be overcome by the resources of the microfilm camera and the electronic brain. While the microfilm camera copies or records millions of pages of printed texts, the electronic brain will analyze them and index and cross-index them under appropriate headings.

Tomorrow's researcher, in the comfort of his home or his office, will be able to scan through the pertinent writings in any subject area in a fraction of the time it would otherwise take by simply asking the library's electronic brain to bring forth the answers to any questions. High-speed electronic printers at every microfilm reader will make reproductions of this data immediately available.[22]

This is a beautiful picture of the world of tomorrow, but we are yet a long, long way from its realization.

As one more of the limits for dealing with the problems which supposedly can be solved by proper relationships between man and machine, certainly the matter of how much information there is and will be is most vital. John W. Sanders computed in 1963 that as of 1958, there were "between 750 and 770 million books, pamphlets, journals, maps, and photographs, and so on, in the world's library, and that the total number of bits of information represented by all these items is roughly two quadrillion, which is increasing at the rate of 2 million bits per second." Very appropriately, he calls this "a sobering thought."[23]

In a follow-up of the Sanders article, *Scientific American* stated that:

using Sanders' estimates, it is possible to compare the "information explosion" with the "population explosion" in order to see how man's ability to produce recordable literary works compares with his ability to produce readers. So far readers, potential readers, outnumber books and other library items at least four to one. Moreover, population is increasing at the rate of about two humans per second, compared with one new library item every three seconds.

Nevertheless, the gap is closing; the population is growing at a rate of only about 2 percent per year compared to about 3 percent per year for reportable items.

My favorite philosophers, the Smothers Brothers, have used, in a most illuminating anecdote, some words on one of their more abstruse records that I think are most apropos in connection with the topic of this paper. Their story tells of how one of the brothers fell into a vat of boiling chocolate and immediately screamed "Fire! Fire!" When asked why he shouted "Fire! Fire!" since obviously there was no fire, he asked sorrowfully, "Would anyone have come to pull me out if I had yelled 'Chocolate! Chocolate!'?" This is about the way I feel about my summer's plunge into the plethora of current library literature on the subject of what the machine is doing to the library or the library to the machine or the interaction of both. Just crying, "Machines! Machines!" will not alleviate this flood of material.

I suggest that perhaps what is really needed is at least a brief breathing-space period, during which those of us who have the common sense to admit that the machine is here, whether we much like it or not, can sit back and reflect on the problems attendant on use of the machine without either the superenthusiasm of the fanatic proponent or the superdolorousness of the rabid opponent to mar our attempts at objective ratiocination.

The machine and the library will become a team in some future day, both for data processing and for information retrieval, the first, of course, much sooner than the second. Until that day, we who are living during the first or early stages of library mechanization must expect to have problems and difficulties. There will be no dramatic breakthrough, at least in my pessimistic view, and at best, some of the objections so vividly voiced by Wasserman and others must be kept in mind.

## GOOD-BYE, REFERENCE LIBRARIANS!

The funeral ceremonies are over, the usual "few nice words" have been said, and so good-bye, Reference Librarian!

The documentalists said a not too fond farewell years ago. Their unseemly haste was the to be expected concomitant of a rather shaky set of premises, wobbliest of which was the oft-repeated but never "documented" asseveration that the coming of the computer and other electronic data-processing equipment would necessarily mean the demise of the old-fashioned human reference librarian and his replacement by a clanking, light-flashing, information-spouting retrieval machine. An occasional drop of oil and a few twists of a nut here and a lifting of a lever there would be all that was needed—aside from, of course, such trivia as machine operators, information retrieval specialists, and patrons capable of understanding and using the peculiar, esoteric lingua franca of the documentalists.

Now the librarians, and most horrendous of all, even the library schools, are beginning to play their parts toward the interment of the reference librarian. In the Spring, 1964, issue of *Library Resources and Technical Services,* there is a summary article on "Technical Services in 1963," in which we are told that "the library schools are responding to the developments in the field [of documentalism], even though there may be some question as to just what is the best approach to meet the demands of 'technical people.'" Don R. Swanson, dean of the University of Chicago's Graduate Library School, is preparing "a program of 'information science' on the Ph.D. level which will 'include calculus, modern algebra, logic, applied math, information theory and computer organization and design,'" as well as "'certain courses in the field of linguistics and possibly in psychology.'"[24]

Some antidote to this rather still stiff proposed dose for our prospective reference librarians comes in Frances Neel Cheney's recent report on "The Teaching of Reference in American Library Schools." She stresses that, at least for the "modest beginning course," all indications are that the "long-established corpus of information . . . will continue to serve in all types of libraries and at all levels."[25]

In the same issue Katherine G. Harris, writing of "Reference Service Today and Tomorrow: Objectives, Practices, Needs, and Trends," agrees with the documentalists that "the implications of machine storage and retrieval of information, particularly in the fields of science and technology, are . . . vast"; but she insists that it is the doing of routine clerical tasks which is "the point at which automation will develop most profitably in libraries." For her—and this sounds blessedly familiar and completely accurate (if not "scientific") to me—"the reference function of a library is concerned with the collection and organization of informational materials and efficient use, assisting readers in using the materials, answering requests for information in person or by telephone, and preparing lists or bibliographies for research when time permits."[26]

It is good to know that the documentalists themselves are having some second thoughts on their raison d'être. An article in the April, 1963, issue of *American Documentation* gives some very cogent arguments to prove that "the geometrical rate of increase in scientific and technological publications raises no particular problems, does not create any particular threatening situations, and does not require crash programs." Indeed, the writer says that "the attitude which sees in mechanization the only hope of solving the impending crisis in information retrieval is objectively unjustified and subjectively danger- ous, because it tends to replace dispassioned scientific analysis by wishful thinking and therefore diverts valuable research time into utopian speculations." The author admits that "partial mechanization of various aspects of the information-retrieval field is theoretically feasible, but its economic feasibility can be determined only by extensive research and experimentation."[27]

It is very good to know that this advice has been taken by the doyen of libraries, the Library of Congress. As the result of a three-year study by a team of seven experts in the areas of business and electronic machines, working for the Library of Congress through the largess of the Council on Library Resources, we now are told that "automation of bibliographic processing, catalog searching, and docu- mentary retrieval is technically and economically feasible in large research libraries." Of course, there is a little matter for the Library of Congress alone of spending about $20 million; and if their recom- mendations are to be carried out for a national system, from $50 to $70 million will be required. However, it perhaps would be salutary to mention that in their report it is explicitly stated that "the retrieval of the intellectual content of books by automatic methods is not now feasible for large collections." So, another reprieve for the harried reference librarian has been received, perhaps just in time.

Seven years ago a hit Broadway play (later a Katharine Hepburn- Spencer Tracy movie), *Desk Set*, reduced the notion of the com- pletely automated library to sufficient absurdity, one would think, to scotch the notion for at least our time. Certainly there are routine activities in any type of larger library which should be handled mechanically. But does this mean that reference work, as defined above by Harris, is to be turned over in toto to the computer and the IBM Selector?

Reference work, after all, still involves reason and judgment. No computer yet made can reason, and its capacity for judgment is on the most elementary levels. Maybe that "Good-bye, Reference Li- brarian!" may yet turn to a "Hello, Reference Librarian: Where Have You Been Hiding?"

## THE IRRELEVANCE OF RELEVANCE

Every generation seems to have its "in" word, and certainly "relevance" is the word to conjure with these days. No matter what aspect of life is being discussed, someone is bound to bring up the seemingly vital question, "is it relevant?" Very rarely, indeed, is there a clarification of just what would happen if the particular matter under discussion were *ir*relevant. For that matter, relevant to what?

Many years ago Robert Lynd, the author of *Middletown,* wrote a rather profound study of the relevance of social research to the world as it then was, under the rubric, *Knowledge for What?* Perhaps I can paraphrase that to ask, and really not be facetious about it, "relevance for what?" The modern library—school, academic, or public—is under a fantastic pressure from those who seem to be living just for today to design their libraries in terms entirely of today's problems, with the idea that the only thing that can answer today's problems are today's answers. In my judgment, this is (to use what has seemed to be a favorite word in "Overdue" lately) garbage! But to get back to my theme.

In the last two years, a great deal of *over*attention seems to me to have been paid to problems that certainly deserve their due share of consideration but have no business getting in the way of the normal, everyday responsibilities of libraries. In the academic library, the falling-over-in-a-faint because of the need for black studies materials is perhaps my best example. I will defer to no one in the library profession in the work that I have done and the responsibility I have shown, on a national level, in getting the American Library Association and libraries in general to be responsive to the demonstrated needs of minority groups in this country. But the majority *does* exist, or to put it more sensibly, perhaps, there are a great many minorities, and all of them have their problems. The racket which has developed among even comparatively sober and stable publishing companies in rushing into publication of "original" and scissors-and-paste jobs and reprints on the subject of black history and black literature is a notorious blot on that particular escutcheon. But I can't understand why libraries, mainly run by rather sober and responsible people, should become so panic-stricken because they don't have enough books on black studies to support the course, or information about the black minority, when they also certainly lack books on a great many other vital topics.

I happen to be one of a minority which has had its share of being ignored and defamed and which has had its share of abuse, even though obviously in this country, at least, not on the level endured by the blacks. But I have not yet heard that there is a national drive for Jewish studies nor that there are fantastic publishing schemes for reproducing *all* of the material on Jewish history or literature that seems relevant—good, bad, or indifferent though it may be in quality.

Relevant. There's that word again. George S. Counts, who in his day was one of the most influential professors of education in the United States, in 1962 talked about some of the "foundations of human freedom." He said that education should be used "to inculcate a deep love of liberty." He asked that there be a basic responsibility in education to "honor this basic moral principle worth the dignity of the individual." He asked that there be "toleration of and respect for differences—differences of opinion and thought." And, finally, he asked for "the encouragement of the critical mind."

Somehow we are finding that this is going by the board. Criticism has been replaced by abuse and reason by emotion if, for example, the activities of some at the Atlantic City ALA Conference is any example. In the same little volume previously quoted, *Education and the Foundations of Human Freedom,* Counts quotes from a statement made by Arthur Balfour, which Counts says should serve as a guide for any education designed to serve the cause of freedom under law:

It matters little what other gifts a people may possess if they are wanting in those which, from this point of view, are of most importance. . . . If, for example, they have no capacity for grading their loyalties as well as being moved by them; if they have no natural inclination to liberty and no natural respect for law; if they lack good humor and tolerate foul play; if they know not how to compromise or when; if they have not that distrust of extreme conclusions which is sometimes mis-described as want of logic; if corruption does not repel them; and if their divisions tend to be either too numerous or too profound, the successful working of British institutions may be difficult if not impossible.

With only one revision, and that is to say that the successful working of *American* institutions might be equally "difficult, if not impossible," I offer Balfour's words as a guide for librarians as well as for other educators.

This whole recent movement toward librarians as being the exact equivalent of social reformers is a little too shrill and unreasonable for me. I would like to have someone explain to me just how and why suddenly we became the movers and shakers of the American body politic. I am somehow reminded of Rostand's Chanticleer, the rooster who had the rather odd notion that every time he crowed at morn, this caused the sun to rise.

## NOTES

1. This section is based on a talk given to the Midwest Academic Librarians Conference on May 7, 1976, at the University of Northern Iowa, Cedar Falls, Iowa.

2. Glenn Tinder, *Tolerance: Toward a New Civility* (Amherst: University of Massachusetts Press, 1976), p. 138.

3. Ibid., p. 141.

4. Dorothy Nelkin, "The Science-Textbook Controversies," *Scientific American* (April, 1976), pp. 33-39.

5. James G. Martin, *The Tolerant Personality* (Detroit: Wayne State University Press, 1964), p. 119.

6. Aleksandr Nikitenko, *The Diary of a Russian Censor* (Amherst: University of Massachusetts Press, 1975).

7. Based on Paul Cors, "Academic Libraries and Intellectual Freedom," in American Library Association Office for Intellectual Freedom, *Intellectual Freedom Manual* (Chicago: ALA, 1974), part 3, pp. 14-16.

8. James Madison, *Letters and Other Writings,* vol. 3, 1816-1828 (Philadelphia: Lippincott, 1865), pp. 276-81.

9. Paul Wasserman, *The Librarian and the Machine* (Detroit: Gale Research, 1965).

10. Ibid., p. 29.

11. Ibid., p. 30.

12. Ibid., pp. 30-31.

13. Ibid.

14. Ibid., p. 31.

15. Ralph R. Shaw, "The Form and the Substance," *Library Journal* (February 1, 1965), pp. 567-71.

16. Donald P. Hammer, "Automated Operations in a University Library: A Summary," *College and Research Libraries* (January, 1965), pp. 19-29, 44.

17. "Library Statistics of Colleges and Universities 1963-64: Institutional Data," U.S. Office of Education, circular no. 769, OE-15023-64 (Washington, D.C.: Government Printing Office, 1965), p. 21.

18. Gretchen W. Koriagin, "Experience in Man and Machine Relationships in Library Mechanization," *American Documentation* (July, 1964), pp. 227-29.

19. Verner W. Clapp, "Research and Problems of Scientific Information in Retrospected Prospect," *American Documentation* (January, 1963), pp. 1-9.

20. Simon M. Newman, "Information Retrieval: Toward an Ultimate System," 88th Cong., 1st sess., National Information Center, Committee on Education and Labor, House of Representatives, appendix to vol. 1, pts. 1-3, pp. 449-52.

21. Frederick P. Keppel, "Looking Forward: A Fantasy," in *The Library of Tomorrow*, ed. Emily Miller Danton (Chicago: American Library Association, 1939), pp. 1-11.

22. Maurice B. Mitchell, "A Forward Look at Communication," *Britannica Book of the Year, 1958* (Chicago: Encyclopaedia Britannica).

23. John W. Sanders, "Information Storage Requirements for the Contents of the World's Libraries," *Science* (September 13, 1963), pp. 1067-68.

24. Maurice Tauber, "Technical Services in 1963," *Library Resources and Technical Services* (Spring, 1964), pp. 101-111.

25. Frances Neel Cheney, "The Teaching of Reference in American Library Schools," *Journal of Education for Librarianship* 3, no. 3 (Winter, 1963), pp. 188-98.

26. Katherine G. Harris, "Reference Service Today and Tomorrow: Objectives, Practices, Needs and Trends," *Journal of Education for Librarianship* 3, no. 3 (Winter, 1963), pp. 188-98.

27. Yehoshua Bar-Hillel, "Is Information Retrieval Approaching a Crisis?" *American Documentation* (April, 1963), pp. 95-98.

# 3 THE DAY'S WORK

## BROWSING AT ISC LIBRARY

As in most modern college libraries, Idaho State College Library has a room specifically planned for recreational reading. The Browsing Room, located in the front northeast corner of the building, is an oak-floored, comfortably and tastefully decorated room with inviting soft chairs and book-lined walls.

Here students and faculty may relax and enjoy some 1,100 volumes, both hard bound and paper covered, intended to serve as a restful adjunct to the study-directed contents of the rest of the library. Throughout the day and evening, most of its thirty seating places are usually occupied, and quiet conversation and cigarette smoking are both permitted.

Approximately thirty to fifty of the Browsing Room books circulate daily, with a seven-day loan period being imposed to permit wide circulation of the popular books here. There is no separate librarian or attendant; the books are selected by the librarian, and the shelving taken care of by the circulation department. If a patron wishes to take one of the Browsing Room books out, he or she brings the book to the central circulation desk, located about fifteen feet from the entrance to the Browsing Room.

One of the regular features of the Browsing Room is the institution known as the Browsing Room Book Tea. These teas have been held in the library Browsing Room on Thursday afternoons at 4 P.M., from October through April, for some six years now. The speakers are faculty members who have interesting stories to tell of hobbies or trips or anything else of a fairly light nature which is not directly connected with their specialty. Often slides are shown, and there has even been a Hawaiian hula dance (performed by a Hawaiian student to help illustrate a talk on a trip to Hawaii by a professor of education). Some of the topics of typical book teas have been "Yellowstone Yarns," "Science Fiction and Fact," "A Yank at Oxford," "The Compleat Desert Rat," and "Hi-Fi—Why?"

Tea is prepared and served by a committee of Associated Women Students, and ten cents is charged to defray the cost of tea, cookies, lemon, and sugar. Proceeds, if any, are used each year to purchase books of particular interest to college women, as selected by a committee composed of the AWS committee and the librarian. As a general rule, approximately twenty dollars is usually available for this purpose each year, and the books purchased are marked with gift plates indicating their source. Attendance at these teas includes students, faculty, and townspeople, with thirteen Browsing Room Book Teas being held during 1954-55, and a total attendance recorded of 291. Eight books were purchased from the money available at the end of the season.

To return to the makeup of the Browsing Room collection, it should be noted that approximately $200 per year is spent on books specifically ordered for this room. Selections are made from such lists as "Fifty Notable Books of the Year" and the "Gold Star List of Fiction." The books are shelved in alphabetical author order, with the exception of various small tabletop displays which are changed from time to time. These are on such topics as "Fascinating Women," "U.S.A.," and "Think a Little."

Separate shelves are also maintained for science fiction, mystery stories, westerns, poetry, humor, cartoon books, art and photography, sports, and short stories. The general intention is to act as somewhat of a "public library" to busy college students and faculty members. There has even been established a Faculty Shelf, with books on such topics as high fidelity, education, and college fiction.

Campus use of the Browsing Room is about as heavy as could be expected, but the attendance at the teas is not as yet proportionately high enough in terms of students. Various steps will be taken this fall to publicize these teas and promote attendance by students, as well as by faculty members.


## FACULTY-LIBRARY COOPERATION

To speak of the cooperation of college faculty and college librarians is, these days, to speak of one of the clichés of college life. If the library is the "heart of the college," as is so commonly said, then surely the heart *must* cooperate with its brains, its voice, its . . . but let me not carry this physiological metaphor to impossible extremes. The fact remains that most members of most college faculties and most college librarians nowadays *do* try to cooperate in achieving the aims of the college—and I have no intention of telling this knowledgeable audience what those are.

But the history of the early days of universities reveals quite a different picture. To begin with, before Gutenberg's time there were very few materials available for reading and study. The scholar of the twelfth through the fifteenth centuries carried his knowledge in his head; Oliver Goldsmith's famous description of the schoolmaster in "The Deserted Village" was all too accurate: "And still they gazed, and still the wonder grew/That one small head could carry all he knew."

As books were costly and few, the early university rented them, at so much per quire. A 1286 document of the University of Paris, for instance, lists for rent copies of 138 different books.[1] After all, books had to be copied by hand, and renting meant not only added income for the universities but also that poor students would be unlikely to walk off with their texts.

Yet students then, like students now, had ways of getting around bureaucratic rules. So, gradually, small accumulations of self-owned libraries grew up, perhaps like Chaucer's "clerk of Oxenford," who was described as preferring "twenty bokes clad in blak or reed" to rich robes or wine. These students, once they in turn became professors, thus had some books, which they could eventually leave as bequests to the colleges. These books the colleges could permit to be borrowed or read in the library.

For libraries there were, even before printed books, of course. The oldest known catalog of the Sorbonne in Paris, dated 1338, lists some 1,722 volumes.[2] King's Hall, predecessor of Trinity College, Cambridge, was begun in 1317, at which time King Edward II gave "certain books of the laws and canons" to King's Hall Library. After Calais was taken in 1347, King Edward III sent three manuscripts, taken from Calais, to King's Hall. King Henry VI, in 1475, presented seventy-seven books to King's Hall. But not only kings stocked their shelves; the records reveal many, many volumes donated by former students and by faculty members.[3]

Surely faculty could go no further in cooperation than actually to furnish the foundations of the library, the books themselves. On the whole, however, books played a secondary role to the words of the professor, even more secondary than in those colleges of today in which the lecture system of medieval days survives, almost unaltered in most respects.

The early history of American colleges makes few references to college libraries, probably because of their very minor importance in those days. Most early American college librarians, in such institutions as Harvard, William and Mary, Princeton, Brown, and Dartmouth, had been educated for the ministry and had their principal occupation as college instructors, with the work of being "library keepers" just one more added task.

It is by now a well-established story that Mr. Sibley, a nineteenth-century Harvard librarian, once completed an inventory and was subsequently seen crossing Harvard Yard smiling very happily. When asked why, he replied, "Every book in the library is on the shelves but two; Agassiz has those, and I am on my way now to get them." Whether literally true or not, this attitude was certainly typical among the so-called watchdog librarians, whose main object was, as has been said, "to keep the books in and the noisy students out."[4]

And not only students. No one really was able to make much use of these libraries, for the early American college libraries had few books and even fewer hours during which to use or get them. Just before the Revolutionary War, according to the same authority, Amherst and Trinity libraries were open once a week, from 1 to 2 P.M., and the Princeton Library was open one hour twice a week. In its early days the library of the University of Missouri was open only a single hour every two weeks.

Even so late as 1870, the notion that a college library was the sole concern of the college librarian remained prevalent; witness Columbia College, as vast Columbia University was called then. Books could be withdrawn only during a specified ninety-minute period each weekday; the librarian, on the authority of the reminiscences of each of the professors, "generally seemed displeased when anyone asked for a book and positively forbidding when asked to buy one."[5] After all, books cost money and took a good deal of work to process and care for.

It would be nice if I could say, "Those days are gone forever!" An honest appraisal of what goes on in college libraries the country over would, however, show that most college libraries today are run on far different principles. Ideally, perhaps the college library now should function as stated a few years ago by Carl White, today's Columbia University director of libraries: "We ought to act as a catalytic agent, bringing together the human being and the book and then disappearing as the reaction occurs, again to appear to bring the next human being and the next book together."[6] The pejorative "Oh, yeah?" which may be your personal reaction to this rather fanciful picture may possibly be counteracted if you will pay heed to a few details indicating how this admittedly difficult ideal may at least approach realization.

To begin with, in considering this matter of college education, the book, the librarian, the student, and the faculty member, perhaps it might be wise to see what the ideal faculty member should be like. Ordway Tead in 1950 told the Conference on Improving the Effectiveness of College Faculties that the following were the attributes of the model college teacher:

He or she is committed to transmitting through a specific discipline all of his own awareness of the *best* that he knows—the best intellectually, esthetically, spiritually. He is charged passionately to carry forward and pass on the torch of the finest human learning. He has also to interpret all this in terms of the need and desire of today's young people as they themselves see their world and grope for satisfactions. He is sufficiently creative to enlarge and make ever more meaningful that knowledge and wisdom of which he is possessed. He is helping the young *to know, to value, to aspire, to achieve, to believe,* in terms that he has himself found productive in confronting life's perplexities.

This paragon of a teacher will know with high confidence his own hierarchy of values—be it in fields artistic, political, economic, scientific, sociological, literary, spiritual. He will realize that the values to be clarified and given living power stem not alone from one cultural source—namely, the Hellenistic-Judeo-Christian—but from many in a global and universalistic frame. He will know the central dialectic of reason and faith, of fact and possibility regarding the American heritage, without becoming chauvinistic or being purely occidental in grasp and sympathy. If he is technological or scientific in training, he will know that his own key to truth is vital but not all-inclusive. If he is humanistic, literary, or economic in training, he will be solicitous to discover and interpret a unifying, integrative basis for reflection and action which can help men to see and apply their many discrete bodies of knowledge in some orderly way which makes sense either in rational terms or in some ultimate appeal to a faith frankly recognized to be beyond knowledge.[7]

To deal with this all-wise purveyor of wisdom, it might be well to fashion a college librarian, also on the ideal side. He or she, to paraphrase Tead's statement, must be committed to transmitting through many disciplines all the world's knowledge. Certainly he must understand teaching and its problems. He must have scholarly training and, if possible, achievement, to enable him to cope with scholars. He must view technical processes, terminology, and routines as merely means to an end—the building up and maintaining of a library adapted to the best interests of the library's users.

Since the time of Bacon, few—a very few—men have taken all knowledge for their province. Yet, in a peculiar sense, this must be the aim of the college librarian. He must, if he does not *know*, at least know *where* the knowledge is. Archibald MacLeish once called the librarian "the hat check boy in the parcel room of culture."[8] Surely this is by no means an ignoble function, and, if properly pursued, may furnish a distinct and vital service, deserving, perhaps, of as much effort and preparation as the partaking of the feast.

I promised you details rather than glittering generalities. Let us now see what the librarian can do for the faculty member and, as I am sure you anticipated, what the faculty member can do for the librarian and the library.

If it is granted that the library is a teaching instrument, then it must also be granted that both the library staff and the professor have responsibilities in seeing to it that the library is a good teaching instrument. There are five ways, I suggest, in which the college library functions as such.

In the first place, the library should be an extension of the instructional activities of the classroom. The library provides materials for reserve; houses books; and makes available such materials and services as microfilms, films, pamphlets and so on; has reading areas for special types of materials, including documents, reference books, and periodicals; provides carrels and other reading facilities and conference or seminar rooms; and makes available bibliographic service, exhibits and displays, typing rooms, and faculty research rooms.

In order to help synchronize classwork with library study, the faculty member should know what is in the library from firsthand experience, should plan assignments in advance, using syllabi and book lists (copies of which should be available in the library), should be sure that appropriate materials are in the library before making study assignments, and should take into account the varying abilities of students to find and use library materials.

Several possible means can be used to allow for these unequal abilities. One is to recommend that students do everything they can to learn more about the library and its use. Another is to spell out the details in an assignment, in such ways as giving the call numbers and brief annotations for each item listed.

Another way to help the library supplement the classroom is to have librarians visit classes and discuss with them the best ways of using the library in order to carry out the purposes of that particular class. Librarians may well attend departmental and other meetings when curricular changes are being discussed, to advise on present or potential library resources available for new or altered courses.

The second way in which the college library may function as a teaching instrument is in serving as a laboratory in which the student may develop the ability to use tools of learning. There are two ways in which the faculty may help in this respect. First, as suggested a moment ago, students may be advised by the faculty to take whatever formal courses of library instruction are available. Second, special lectures or demonstrations may be given by librarians, either in the library or in the classroom to help in the proper use of specific library materials needed for a course. The library staff's role in this "laboratory" function is to offer individual aid in helping the research work of students and faculty and to offer bibliographic help.

Third among the ways in which the college library may serve as a teaching instrument is in serving as a source of information on nonacademic subjects. By publicizing books on literary and other cultural subjects, by keeping in touch with current affairs, and by developing worthwhile reading habits, the library is improving the general educational tone of the college and its members. Here the faculty may help by example and by recommendation rather than by assignment, as with academic subjects.

The fourth teaching function of the college library is as a reservoir of knowledge. The well-functioning college library may assist the faculty to increase its efficiency by such means as displaying announcements of graduate courses elsewhere, routing magazines, abstracting or at least listing important professional periodical articles otherwise likely to be overlooked, sending out new book notices, assembling curricular material from other colleges, and keeping a clipping file on important higher education news. The library staff should be both willing and able to help faculty committees, particularly with bibliographic and reference aid. Here the faculty may best cooperate by pointing out gaps in the library's holdings and services which may be filled.

Lastly, in this list of ways in which the college library may serve as a teaching instrument, is as an aid in developing social responsibility among students. The modern open-stack library, with its great temptations for the less scrupulous, is in somewhat the position of the Irish convents during the Middle Ages, as told about by George Moore in his Rabelaisian *A Story-Teller's Holiday.* According to Moore, the nuns deliberately shared their virginal beds with handsome young men in order to prove their true virtue, since without temptation it really was impossible to tell if one was good enough to resist it! I shall leave the results of this noble experiment to your own literary researches to determine, but the analogy to the open library is there.[9]

All of these suggestions have been from the library viewpoint. You may be interested in a study made for the Association of American Universities in 1926 by a college administrator and former professor, George A. Works, of the University of Illinois. In studying a selected group of college and university libraries, Works states that a "deliberate attempt was made to locate some of the most outspoken faculty critics of the library." He went on to say, "Usually this was not difficult."[10]

Works described three primary functions of the college library. These were:

(1) Facilitate and encourage research at least to the extent of securing the necessary printed resources when practicable. This statement

is always subject to the reservation that the lines of research for which materials are being gathered are in harmony with the objectives of the institution. . . . (2) Facilitate the work of teacher and student in the processes of teaching and learning . . . (3) Offer opportunities for the general "cultural" reading of student body and faculty.[11]

It is an interesting sidelight, in connection with the first of these suggested functions, that Works proposes that colleges should pay the travel expenses of faculty who find their needed library materials in other libraries. He believed this would be less expensive than trying to stretch the college library's holdings to suit everyone. Perhaps such advances as bibliographical centers, faster interlibrary loans, and even the use of teletype, as in several Midwestern colleges and universities today, might change his mind.

One very frequently discussed topic, when dealing with faculty-library relations, is the oft-argued one of "Which is more useful, a departmentalized or centralized library?" Works offers, as a general principle for liberal arts colleges, that "a central library should be all that is necessary aside from small collections temporarily lent to departments."[12] He points out, however, that

librarians and administrative authorities should recognize that faculty members will do their best research and teaching only when they are relatively free from irritation. It is better to wait for some time than to slow up the productive work of an individual or a department by an abrupt invasion of what the individual or the department regards as its library prerogatives, unless there is serious interference of the rights of other individuals or departments.[13]

Speaking of faculty "irritation," Works lists the following as most commonly cited by these "outspoken critics" referred to earlier. Faculty, thirty years ago, were bothered by the length of time periodicals were away for binding, particularly if periodicals were not readily accessible during the period of preparation for binding. They felt, also, that library catalogers should study the needs of those making most use of materials before making any seemingly arbitrary classification.

Faculty members in the 1920s were also annoyed by the length of time it took for the library to move in its ponderous fashion to order and get books. Many said that they could not understand why they could write to a publisher and get a book in a few days while the library took weeks for the same order.[14]

Of course, then and now, there are answers and explanations for these recurrent problems. Possibly reference to some pertinent remarks about British faculty-library problems by an Englishman writing in 1947 may give a fresh perspective to what seems to be a universal problem, at least in academic circles the world over:

> Separation has also resulted from the expansion of university work in recent years—the separation between the teacher and the administrator. In all faculties, degree-courses are not only more numerous but more complex than they were forty years ago, with the result that university registries demand the whole-time services of a highly efficient body of officials. Complaints are heard, in consequence, that the modern university is dominated by a group of bureaucrats who delight in drafting, and in administering, complicated regulations for their own sake. Such complaints may be healthy and are certainly inevitable; but they can be of little avail.
>
> For as the number of faculties, and of departments of faculties is continually increasing, a corresponding growth in the personnel of administrative staffs must necessarily follow. Thus it has become one of the major problems of academic life to cope effectively with the wide expansion of knowledge and at the same time to preserve some kind of fundamental unity of purpose which may transcend all diversities of aims and outlook and occupation. Very great importance has recently been attached to "the atmosphere of an association of men and women which takes all knowledge as its province and in which all branches of learning flourish in harmony." These are brave words. But association, if it is to be of value, must be intimate rather than casual, and harmony depends on the possession of something in common. What is there, ultimately, in common between the library and the laboratory, between the bureaucrat and the scholar, between members of a university as a whole?[15]

Let us turn from this gloomy dilemma, to which I am afraid I can offer no comprehensive or pat solution, to consider what I believe to be the *extreme* example of faculty-library cooperation, which could probably be adduced at Stephens College, a private junior college for women with an enrollment of about 2,200. Librarians at Stephens, we are told:

are not a separate group but are working members of the instructional staff. For example, the college librarian has a double position as dean of instruction and librarian. By virtue of this fusion of function, he is encouraged to keep the contribution of the library to teaching constantly before the faculty. Not only the librarian but all members of the professional library staff are members of the instructional staff.[16]

The idea of library-instructional integration has gone so far at Stephens that divisional libraries have been developed near the offices and classrooms of teachers, smaller classroom libraries have been introduced, and conference rooms have been built into the library so the teachers may have at hand those books both they and their students need.[17] Of course, there is no single college library in such a situation; instead, there is a continually changing number of libraries, some temporary, some permanent, intended to keep pace with the experimental pace of this college. It may be noted, however:

Although the libraries are decentralized in location they are centrally administered. Ordering and cataloging of books for all college libraries are done in a single department. In addition to catalogs in each permanent library, a union catalog of the holdings of all libraries is maintained in a central library.[18]

The general library of Stephens College includes, in addition to the union catalog, the following:

Periodical indexes, bound volumes of periodicals, a general reference collection, a loan collection of more than five hundred framed color reproductions of noted pictures for withdrawal and hanging in student dormitory rooms, a collection of three thousand phonograph recordings, and some thirty thousand books in such fields as literature, religion, fine and practical art, music, travel, biography, and history. Next door to the reading room is the catalog and order department. Near the record collection is a listening room where records are played. Adjacent to the literature stacks are five conference rooms where the literature courses of the college are taught.[19]

It is impossible within a brief space to describe in any detail the practically revolutionary nature of the use by Stephens College of the library and library resources. Librarians at Stephens participate actively in faculty work through such media as course outlines, workshops, departmental meetings, informal conferences, class visits, and indeed as actual teachers, even though not in the classroom. Dr. Johnson states:

It is not a passive role that the librarian plays, content to be a passer-out of books, a checker-up of overdues, or just a looker-on in the classroom. She makes an active and positive contribution to the instructional program of the College. She recognizes as one of her most important obligations the training of students themselves to use the library efficiently. She is essentially a teacher as she helps a student define her problem, weigh various approaches to its solution, and finally select and locate helpful materials for study. The librarian is teaching effectively when she helps a reader identify and point up her interests and select materials to satisfy, deepen, and expand such interests. What is more, she has the important opportunity for teaching at the particular time the student is most actively feeling the need for help—a real psychological advantage.[20]

Of course, the teaching activities of Stephens College librarians are not limited to work in the library. There are many occasions on which a type of cooperative teaching is carried out between the librarian and teacher. Under this system, the librarian occasionally teaches sections of a course during selected units in the librarian's special field of competence. In other words, if a librarian has a special subject background, he or she is able to make use of it in combination with his or her bibliographical background.

Librarians act as substitute instructors when regular instructors are ill at Stephens. Sometimes, Johnson says:

Librarians have assumed complete responsibility for courses in such fields as communications, literature, sociology, and science. In two cases, social studies and literature, librarians who have taught classes have become so interested in teaching that they have eventually transferred to classroom teaching. Having as members of the teaching staff instructors who were formerly librarians has contributed materially to the development of a library-minded faculty, and, incidentally, these librarians have become outstanding teachers.[21]

I am not by any means recommending this extreme among experimentations in library-faculty cooperation; what I am suggesting is that there are possibilities far beyond the usual, well-beaten paths which we have all traveled. It is by no means unlikely that, given the opportunity to review calmly and dispassionately some of the suggestions embodied in this very sketchy report, both faculty members and librarians may see not just a few but many opportunities for improving the work of the college.

The chancellor of Vanderbilt University, Harvie Branscomb, once said, "The natural enemy of the librarian is the professor." I strongly deny this, particularly the adjective. If any professor has become the enemy of the librarian, it is not a matter of nature but of circumstance. As a librarian, I offer the extended hand of fellowship in what is after all our chief concern, the higher education of the youth of America.

## GET-'EM-ALL THEORY

Huzzas to LeRoy Merritt for his spirited, if brief, criticism of the "growing tendency among large public and university libraries to acquire books *en bloc*."[22] Granted that we are in an age of expedience and hurry, surely no self-respecting professional librarian would claim that the purchase of any publisher's offerings without realistic appraisal of each volume makes any sense. We are relinquishing a very important share of our professional obligation, it seems to me, when we order so many "University of Blank Press" volumes. With all due respect to the generally high quality of university press publications, surely there must be some reason why so many of their items get remaindered. To order books as if they are so many sausages seems so ridiculous, on the face of it, that one wonders how large libraries, supposedly staffed by the top people in our profession, are more and more succumbing to the delusion that quantity somehow will bring quality and appropriateness. I, for one, certainly hope that this fantastic enterprise of trying to achieve "completeness" will not lure any of the smaller colleges or public library systems into similar ventures.

On the assumption that there is some logical basis behind such activities as those of the Philadelphia Public Library, the Ohio State

University Library, and others in buying books by publisher rather than according to need, I would be very happy to see a reasoned defense in the *Library Journal* in the future by an appropriate practitioner of the "get-'em-all" theory.

In the June 1 *Library Journal*, Lee Gregory wrote: "What we must do in order to survive is to counteract the abuses of mass communication and try to preserve a sense of values based upon quality, not quantity." In my opinion, the college librarian who orders books as if they were so many sausages; who, for the sake of a doubtful saving in money or time, buys all the output of any publisher without regard for the real needs of his institution, has no sense of values.

True, there are voices heard to the contrary. In the same issue of the *Library Journal*, Robert E. Kingery, chief of the Preparations Division at New York Public Library, said: "For many libraries, books are self selecting once they are known to exist and their precise subject has been determined." This may be true for libraries with the budget of the New York Public Library, but let us look at the financial facts of life of the typical American college library.

Most statistical studies I have seen agree that the typical book budget for the college library nowadays is in the vicinity of $25,000 per year. For this amount, let's say the library can purchase about 5,000 volumes—about 4,000 titles, allowing for multivolume sets and necessary duplications. For 1959, publishing figures show that about 800 American publishing houses issued 14,876 new titles. Of these, there were 382 so-called major publishers (five or more titles and not including "vanity" presses) who issued 13,406 new titles.

There were forty-five active university presses in 1959, which issued 1,389 titles. Should the small or even medium-sized college library give "blanket" orders for 35 percent of the 4,000 titles it can afford? . . . The fact that the Ohio State University faculty one year "ordered more than 90 per cent of the total output from 47 university presses" is hardly a useful guideline for the typical college library.

At my own college, I have the needs of twenty-eight academic departments, with 200 faculty members, ranging in interest from art to zoology, to fill. I have the perpetual task of trying to catch up on out-of-print books, which now are needed. I must attempt to give our 2,500 students that "Reading for Life" preparation, in the way of extracurricular reading, of which we hear so much these days. How will "get-'em-all" buying from publishers help fulfill these obligations? If tried at all, it seems to me, the undiscriminating purchase of the complete output of one or more publishers will mean inevitable waste, as well as abdication of the librarian's inescapable responsibilities.

Long ago Melvil Dewey gave as the "scripture" of book selection, "The best reading for the largest number at the least cost." This, of course, was stated for public libraries, but correctly interpreted, it will serve for college libraries as well. Who would question that the college librarian must supply "the best reading"? And who could agree that the best reading is self-selected?

Helen Haines, in her classic text on book selection, *Living with Books*, says to the librarian: "Do not attempt to build up a 'complete' collection; select the best books on a subject, the best books of an author, the most useful volumes of a series, and do not make a fetish of 'full sets' that possess no specific and evident usefulness." Surely *there* is an appropriate criterion for any college librarian to use in book selection. What "specific and evident usefulness" could all the books of any publisher have?

Just possibly, granted almost unlimited funds and a very large clientele, the purchase of the entire list of some of the top publishing houses, or at least all of the books in particular subject fields, would be the right thing to do. But with $25,000 per year to spend on 4,000 titles, how can any truly professional college librarian even consider "getting-'em-all"?

## COOPERATION AMONG IDAHO'S ACADEMIC LIBRARIES

The latest official figures indicate that all of the eleven academic libraries in Idaho—junior college, private college, and university—have an aggregate of less than one million cataloged and classified volumes of books (not including government documents). The magic figure *one million* is the prime requisite for entrance into the select group of the Association of Research Libraries, and Idaho academic collections combined would obviously not qualify for even the entering rung on this significant ladder indicating the top academic libraries of the country.

Idaho's far-flung geography and scattered book collections necessarily require that the academic libraries work together, so far as possible, to see to it that every piece of printed material is used to the fullest. Through the years, many steps have been taken to assure this.

Most recently, the *Union List of Serials,* developed principally by the Idaho State Library, the University of Idaho Library, and the Idaho State University Library, but containing a record of the holdings of all of the major libraries of the state, has been published.

This one item, kept up by annual supplements, will ensure that the periodicals and serials of this state will be made known to all concerned. Many times faculty members and students of various academic institutions have not been aware that within a comparatively few miles, and certainly within reasonable mailing distance, the particular publication they want is available. *The Union List of Serials of Idaho,* which includes both regular publications and Idaho documents, will aid greatly in the provision of reasonably adequate service to the campus communities, in particular, throughout the state.

Another organ of cooperation—this one also quite recent—is the Idaho library teletype network (usually referred to as LITTY), which includes five public libraries, the Idaho State Library, and three academic libraries. The three academic libraries included are the Boise State College Library, the University of Idaho Library, and the Idaho State University Library. These nine institutions are tied together in a network which permits immediate communication. Mostly the matters discussed on this teletype network deal with interlibrary loans. Some reference questions are handled in this way, and occasionally, other matters of a library nature are dealt with. But, in the main, this network is for the purpose of finding out who has what and where, among the major libraries of the state. Those academic libraries which are not themselves members of this network usually use the library nearest them. For example, the College of Idaho at Caldwell generally uses the Boise State College teletype; the Lewis-Clark Normal School generally uses the Public Library at Lewiston; the Ricks College Library normally would use the network connection at Idaho Falls;

the College of Southern Idaho Library uses the Twin Falls Public Library outlet. Literally dozens of calls per day are handled on this network, and since its inception a couple of years ago, it has permitted much more rapid interlibrary communication and particularly the speeding up of the whole interlibrary loan process.

Several years ago an organization was founded which has also served to help cooperation among the academic libraries of this state. This is the Idaho Council of State Academic Libraries, commonly called ICOSAL, which includes the four heads of the state-supported academic libraries. This group of four head librarians meets at least annually and occasionally more often than that. Through the several years it has been in operation, perhaps its most useful achievement has been an agreement to permit the faculty and student bodies of all state-supported institutions to use each other's libraries interchangeably. In other words, it is now a fact that a student who is attending the University of Idaho and who happens to come to Pocatello will get student privileges, while he is here at Idaho State University, just as well as at Lewis-Clark Normal, Boise State, and his own campus, the University of Idaho. The same is true of faculty members from each of the other institutions. All that is necessary is satisfactory identification as either a student or a faculty member of one of the four institutions, and reciprocal privileges are then granted.

The ICOSAL members have also consulted on such matters as budget planning, interchange of publications, uniform schedules, applications for federal grants, statistics, and similar matters. Out of this group eventually will probably come a group which will be representative of all eleven academic libraries in the state, dedicated to similar purposes.

There are, of course, many future possibilities for improvement in academic library cooperation in our book-starved and library-thin state. Some consideration is already being given to the possibilities of central storage of less-used materials in one place, perhaps in Boise at the State Library. Another possibility is centralized processing of materials, as is now being done at Ricks College Library, for some of the public libraries. Still another eventual solution to the lack of books is greatly increased use of specialized collections—so that the University of Idaho Library, for example, might in years to come buy *all* books besides basic ones in fields where it is already strong, such

as law and agriculture, or the Idaho State University Library might
become the state's sole repository of books in the health sciences,
beyond bare curricular needs of each institution.

No doubt, as library technology develops during the next generation, ideas only dimly seen and seemingly impossible to actualize will
become realities. As mechanized methods of information retrieval
come out of the laboratory and the pilot project stages, Idaho
academic libraries will take their place among those using the new
gadgetry. Most of us have discarded quill pens for typewriters, and
there are even some forward-lookers who claim that there are other
ways of communication besides print.

All joking aside, Idaho academic libraries are working hard to
cooperate, and in the very best sense of the word *cooperation,* each
institution is doing its share to try to give the fullest possible library
service to the state's academic community.

## SELLING THE ACADEMIC LIBRARY

The old tradition of the college student as a captive audience for
his institution's library is outdated. In these days of political activism,
multimedia interests, and overcrowded campuses, the library must do
a real selling job or fall behind in the competition for campus
attention. The reserve book room or desk may have its involuntary
devotees, but the use of the rest of the library is more or less
dependent on the quality and quantity of the public relations practiced by the library.[23]

The library? That is a building and its contents. Rather, by the
staff—professional, clerical, and student. Each of these groups has an
appropriate part to play in helping convince the library patron that
he or she must make the library a regular place to visit and use. And
all of the members of the library staff must do all they can to
establish a favorable image of the library by what they *do* rather than
by what the words issued officially from the library *say* they do.

It is of little use to keep talking, in the school's catalog or the
library handbook, about the library as the heart of the college or
university if this is not more than an empty phrase. When an
academic library is really attuned to its institution and its patrons,
and the library staff is made up of trained, devoted people who really

help rather than individuals who concentrate on shushing noisy students and requiring minute observance of finicky rules, public relations are easy. All that a library staff person charged with the specific, official public relations responsibility (and every academic library should have someone so designated) has to do, in the smoothly functioning institution, is to "tell it like it is."

No academic library ever has enough funds or enough staff or enough reading materials or, except perhaps during the first year after a new building or addition is opened, enough space. But every academic library has excellences and services, achievements and timely events, of which even regular library habitués may not be aware. There is no portion of the academic community that has more of general interest to tell and, unfortunately, that usually tells less. And then usually the library tells that little badly.

Basically, the academic library has three audiences—the campus, the general public, and other libraries. The modern academic library, if it is doing its job, should be producing publications and information of value far beyond its walls. Surely, particularly in tax-supported institutions, the tax-paying constituency and the legislature are both entitled to know what the library is doing beyond the routine level. And in private colleges, the alumni are an analogous group, concerned and curious.

Let's be more specific. First, what groups actually on the campus are, or should be, interested in the library? The administration needs to know whenever the library produces a worthwhile bibliography, prepares an absorbing exhibit or display, obtains a useful new library-related machine, performs an unusual service, or receives a gift of some consequence. The faculty and staff, and especially immediately involved departments or services, should be informed of these happenings also, preferably through whatever medium is commonly seen by the faculty and staff. The campus newspaper, an obvious public relations target for the library, should have either a regular library column written by a library staff member or a reporter assigned to the library as his regular beat, if the editor can be so persuaded.

Incidentally, like all other library news releases, whatever is sent out to the campus paper should avoid the didactic and the dull. Perhaps that is not so incidental, either. Today's public is not going to read a dry book review of, say, *The Tergiversations of Anti-monianism* or a similar specialized work. Either write a timely, absorbing comment calculated to be of wide interest, on one or more books, or an appropriate, readable description of a lesser-known library service—or forget it. Save the expository material, dull or not, for handout library manuals or leaflets. These also should be as interestingly written as possible, geared to attract the reader and not likely to be thrown away.

Academic libraries, no matter how many millions are spent on staff and books or palatial buildings, must work toward good public relations with their regular patrons. They must have useful direction signs and understandable card catalog instructions. As has been said, "Eschew esoteric and sesquipedalian verbiage," or more simply, say what you have to say and what needs to be said, then stop.

But don't count on prior knowledge of how to use a library, whether by students or by faculty. In particular, most librarians seem to think that it is not asking too much to expect high school and college graduates to understand the difference between the Dewey Decimal System and the Library of Congress Classification. This is important knowledge to have because many academic libraries are reclassifying. It should not be taken for granted, however, that most patrons understand how to find books in a library with two classification systems. This may appear to most academic librarians as very obvious stuff, but experience in many academic libraries seems to justify bringing public relations down to a very simple level indeed.

Along with the ABC's of public relations go, of course, more advanced ways of telling the library's story. For instance, in every library there are particular excellences. Why not, along with other matters, feature these as part of the regular series of library displays? It is sometimes hard even for the library staff, especially in a large library, to be aware of the wide variety of special collections in the library system. Don't hide that manuscript collection of the writings of a popular author born locally, nor neglect to tell about the complete set of a relatively uncommon reference work that should be made known to all.

Prepare your displays on a planned, coordinated basis. Keep in mind that one closed book looks much like another when set up on display. Use the full panoply of display and exhibit materials that even modest academic libraries have available—pegboards, exhibit cases, bulletin boards, plastic letters. Other devices and tools are procurable in a wide range of complexity and price.

For over a decade, the Idaho State University Library at Pocatello has been presenting a regular series of book and other reading-material displays calculated to interest its campus community in reading matter that it might not otherwise discover. The topics have included current materials; annually recurring celebrations of such events as United Nations Week, National Library Week, Brotherhood Week, and Christmas; and, what has seemed of most interest, celebrations of various anniversaries connected with outstanding individuals and events.

For example, in 1957-58, there were displays commemorating both the Alexander Hamilton bicentennial and the William Blake bicentennial. In 1958-59, there was the celebration of the Theodore Roosevelt centennial and the sesquicentennial of the birth of Abraham Lincoln. In 1959-60, John Dewey's 100th anniversary and Daniel Defoe's 300th anniversary were both commemorated. In 1960-61, the 150th anniversary of the birth of Leo Tolstoi, the 200th anniversary of David Hume's birth, and the 100th anniversary of the beginning of the Civil War were among the displays included. In 1961-62, the library featured the sesquicentennial of the birth of Charles Dickens and the 200th anniversary of the birth of William Cobbett. In 1962-63, Idaho's Territorial Centennial and the fourteenth year of independence of Israel were celebrated in displays.

In 1963-64, there was, of course, the 400th anniversary of William Shakespeare's birth. In addition, a continuation of the Civil War centennial was featured. The 50th anniversary of World War I was the feature of 1964-65, as well as the 100th anniversary of the birth of Henri Toulouse-Lautrec. The bicentennial of the birth of Thomas Malthus was featured in 1965-66, and in 1967-68, there was the 50th anniversary of the beginning of Soviet Russia. The fact that it was 300 years since the death of Rembrandt was observed in 1968-69, and 1969-70 was highlighted by the 100th anniversary of the birth of Mahatma Gandhi.[24]

An infinite number of possibilities for thematic displays can be found, once a display program is decided upon; but in general, displays at Pocatello were of four types—those featuring an anniversary, celebrations of particular "weeks," displays on particular topics of general interest about which materials could not be found by looking in one place in the card catalog, and displays concerning specific library services. As the years went by, some displays were concerned with controversial and currently relevant themes.

A listing of the main and subsidiary library displays in the ISU Library for 1969-70 may be useful:

Tomorrow's Careers
Mahatma Gandhi (100th Anniversary)
Western Books
United Nations Week
That's a No-No! Drugs, Liquor, Marijuana, and Tobacco
The Defense of America: AMB, CBW, etc.
The Arts in Flux: Art, Drama, Music, Film, and Television
Happy Holidays
The End of the Empires
A Feast of Short Stories
The British Museum and its Publications
Prehistoric Fauna and Flora
Brazil: A World in Itself
The Draft
America the Unbeautiful: Why Conservation?
The United States Supreme Court: Center of Controversy
The American University Today

*Humanities*
Christ and Revolution
Thar's Gold in Them Thar Stacks
Books from Down Under
America's Black Writers
Fiction of the 1960s
World of Art
Religion in Turmoil

*Science*
The World Population Explosion
The Sea: Its Poetry and Practicality
Gems, the Uncommon Stones
Sweeteners; the Bitter Pill

*Social Science and Documents*
   The Blacks in American History
   Law Enforcement
   Japan in the World Picture
   United States Wildlife
   India, Feeble Giant
   Brotherhood
   The Far East
   New Life for American Cities
   The American West
   The American Campus
   Help for Small Business
   Air Today and Gone Tomorrow
   The Challenge of Crime
   Come Josephine (Aviation)
   100 Years of the Weather Bureau
*Other Display Topics*
   Smithsonian Institute and the Arts
   United Nations Week
   Today's Isms
   Communism: Theory and Practice
   Christmas in Other Lands
   Winter Sports Scene in Idaho
   Poverty in the United States
   American Foreign Policy
   Latin America
   United States vs. Environmental Degradation
   History of American Labor Unions
   Blacks in American Politics
   Learn All the Rules of Your Favorite Summer Sports
   Nixon's Brain Trust

The technique used in preparing for the display, once a subject was chosen, was simple and direct. To begin with, the library card catalog was consulted for appropriate subjects and cross-references. Second, the current *Books in Print* was consulted for the particular subject, and the books that seemed suitable and were not already in the library were selected. If appropriate, government document sources, the pamphlet file, and periodical indexes were also consulted, as well as specialized bibliographies on the specific topics.

Meanwhile, original posters dealing with the various topics were drawn by a student staff worker so that they would be ready at the time of the displays, which were normally planned to continue for from two to three weeks during the following school year. Announcements of the displays were sent out ahead of time to the local newspaper and to the student campus newspaper, as well as to the weekly campus calendar. A continuing space on the main student bulletin board in the Student Union was used to publicize each current display, under the heading "The ISU Library Presents."

Not all the displays attracted an equal amount of attention; but it was evident, from requests that were made at the time and later, that many of the materials on display were new to the campus reading community. The reading list series—now numbering over fifty—of the ISU Library is based mainly on displays.

The displays are varied in format in several ways. Pegboards, as the locus of each display, are used to exhibit pamphlets, documents, and clippings, not just books. Appropriate magazine and newspaper articles and photographs are clipped from duplicate materials throughout the months before the scheduled dates of each display. Then they are reviewed for timeliness, appropriateness, readability, and appearance. Sometimes one table is used, sometimes two; sometimes one three-section pegboard, sometimes two; occasionally both sides of each panel. Variety is the mode for attracting maximum attention.

Ordinarily all items on display are available immediately for circulation. The ideal display is one with about fifty items originally, all of which circulate before the display period is finished. Incidentally, attractive book jackets are always kept on file for possible use in displays.

The beneficial results of the ISU continuing series of displays are so evident that other academic libraries might well consider at least a modified plan for continuing displays. They decorate the library; they attract readers. They result in the satisfaction of the main drive of any librarian—getting the right books and the right readers together.

Another quite popular means of accomplishing two goals of academic library public relations is through the "Friends of the Library" group. With growing financial pressures on academic administrators,

the possibility of new sources for new library funds is always welcome. And library "friends" groups, which can be organized in a
myriad of ways and for many different purposes, are proving to be a
rather easy means of getting both friends of the library and more
funds or materials for the library.

Perhaps the zenith in American "friends" groups is the one at
Brandeis University, which for many years, through various schemes
for raising money, has provided practically all the regular book
purchase support for the library there. But this is an unusual, probably unique, situation, not likely to be a national model. Still, it
indicates just how far such a group can go if it is dedicated.

More commonly, "friends" organizations, usually composed of
alumni, strive to bring in collections or individual books that the
library needs but is unlikely to get through normal funding channels.
Some academic libraries have found "friends" groups less effective
than direct pleas to the alumni through the regularly published
alumni news. At Idaho State University, the direct approach has
proved quite successful, with the help of effective cooperation from
the alumni director, library staff members, and interested faculty.

If an academic library does sponsor "Friends of the Library," it
should not do so in a token way. Time for planning, provision for at
least annual meetings, and some preliminary expenditure of funds for
literature with which to contact potential members and for mailing
costs are essential.

Another important public relations device for the academic library
is its correspondence. If forms and letters sent out from the library
give the impression that the library conforms to the stereotype in
which a horn-rimmed, dour-visaged spinster sits waiting for the un-
wary patron to violate a piddling rule, the library cannot expect to
be popular. Many libraries that spend much time and money on
internal displays, signs, and publications send out forms and letters
that should be obviously recognizable as counterproductive.

No one expects an academic library to run without reasonable
rules involving such matters as the circulation of books, the hours of
service, interlibrary loans, overdue charges, and so on. But what
faculty member or student is not likely to cut to a minimum his use
of a library that sends curt, jargon-filled notices? Granted that with
the vast student bodies that some major libraries must accommodate,

it is difficult to keep the human touch. Yet such a simple step as revising forms and letters to sound less formal and impersonal would help most academic libraries, of whatever size.

Letters from the library to prospective employees are important, too. Most academic libraries are always engaged in recruiting potentially valuable new staff members, and it is disheartening to see how careless many letters of this type are. (Just as this is being written, the academic library administrator in a nearby county seems to be dealing with a buyer's market, where there are many more qualified applicants than there are openings. Naturally, this has not always been the case, nor is it likely to continue to be so.) But no matter what the state of the library employment market, every applicant, whether his application has been solicited by advertisement or otherwise, or even if it is sent in unsolicited, certainly deserves the courtesy of a personal reply, not a form letter. Each of his specific inquiries should be answered, and he should be sent as much information about the library, the institution, and the community as he seems to deserve in terms of his potential for the specific position or for employment at any time in the future. One never knows when failure to reply personally to a letter may eventually result in bad public relations for the library. But this should not be the motivating factor for what are, after all, the fundamental ingredients of all public relations, simple courtesy and good manners.

The real test of public relations, in the long run, is service. All the elaborately printed and flossily decorated booklists and handbooks, all the news releases, all the displays and signs—these and other more visible examples of dealing with the library's public cannot compare in importance to the way the staff behaves toward patrons. It is ridiculous when an academic institution spends $10 million on its library building, $1 million on furnishings and machines, and vast continuing sums on staff and reading materials, only to have all these made naught by a two-dollar-an-hour student assistant who behaves contemptuously or carelessly to the patron in the library.

It is well worth any academic library administrator's time to be almost as careful in the selection and retention of student and clerical assistants as of professional staff members. The library that willingly accepts the leftover students seeking employment in the university, those students who are neither intellectually nor emotionally suitable for library work, deserves the bad public relations which will almost inevitably result. And inservice training, rather than chance assignment of tasks is the key to a cooperative, well-trained student assistant.

A student library assistant's position should not result in special library privileges. If a book, for example, is on a two-hour reserve, it should not go out for three hours or more to an individual who happens to be on the library staff. The head of the library, too, should observe meticulously every rule that he expects others to observe, or fairness and equity really do not exist in the institution he heads. Surely public relations will suffer, once special privilege becomes known, as it always seems to. This applies even to the treatment of such august individuals as deans and bursars and vice-presidents and even presidents and board members. They may grumble when forced to comply with the rules, but they will appreciate the honest endeavor of the library staff to give everyone an equal opportunity to use the library's resources.

One aspect of academic library public relations that deserves particular mention in these days of "participatory democracy" is the image the library staff presents in its dealings away from the library with students, faculty, and administrative staff. The library staff that becomes ingrown and omphaloskepsistic will not know what its patrons really think about the library and its services, and may take actions contrary to widely expressed needs.

Too often it is the head librarian alone who is known as an active participant in the broader affairs of the institution, and all too often this is the fault of the head librarian. He should encourage active participation in faculty affairs, even including what may be considered to be routine committee meetings. This plea for active participation does presuppose that the professional librarians on any academic library staff are full faculty members—but that is another story! Nonetheless, the professional staff that accepts as a continuing obligation its share in faculty life is much more likely to be accepted as full colleagues by other members of the faculty than the staff that isolates itself.

On sprawling campuses with long distances between the main or branch libraries and such general faculty meeting places as dining rooms and cafeterias, it is a great temptation to librarians to meet and talk with other librarians only. But more goodwill can be engendered in a ten-minute conversation over coffee than can possibly come out of reams of mimeographed, canned publicity.

At the very least, an occasional note or phone call to a faculty member, on a matter that may be of particular interest to him, can be rewarding. There is no need to pester these busy men and women; but there is every need to help them by reminding them of the particular book that has just arrived in their special field, or by asking them for information only their expertise can provide, or in other ways indicating that the library is not simply a collection of closed books. Even auditing or taking an occasional class for credit is an aspect of making the library staff visible, a segment of a good public relations program.

As has been said earlier in another connection, probably the most important single concept in formulating an academic library's public relations program is service. The librarian who forgets that the library is auxiliary to the major function of his institution will not bring books and people together, and any library can lapse into weakened repute if it is not providing timely, efficient, and useful service.

For this reason, the library public relations program, although preferably coordinated by a single individual, should be part of every library department's plan and program. In the small library, it should be handled by the library's head; in the medium-sized library, by an assistant or associate librarian; in the large library, by a trained public relations professional. It should be an active part of every day's operations, whether in reference or circulation or interlibrary loan or acquisitions or cataloging. It can work only if each member of the library staff on every level is constantly doing his share.

The library public relations program is usually divided into three portions: publicity, public relations, and publication. No amount of any one of these will make up for a reasonable presentation of the others, so they all deserve attention.

If the parent institution's news bureau is flooded with reports of trivial library "news," it is unlikely that releases will ever evoke more than "My God, more library stuff!" as a reaction from the news staff. Judicious selection of news of relevance, likely to be of interest to the entire campus community and preferably also to the outside community, will result in the publicity the academic library needs.

As a rule of thumb, if the campus newspaper prints an average of one item a week and the local newspaper one a month, the library is probably getting its fair share of publicity. Not all stories need to be written up in detail by the library's own reporter. If the material to be released has elements of wide interest, call the news bureau and/or the campus paper, ask a reporter to come over to see for himself, and if appropriate, ask a photographer to come along to take pictures of the display or the new book purchase. It is of importance to the whole campus if your library, for example, is computerizing its circulation procedures or its catalog; it is certainly big news if your hours or fine rules are being changed. Remember, undue modesty never will result in due publicity.

Internal public relations are most significant to the success of the library, but they are likely to be given short shrift. Ask any academic library administrator what he is doing for good public relations among the staff, and he will probably wonder what on earth you are talking about. Yet one can walk into almost any academic library, unfortunately, and without prying find unmistakable evidence of alienation between departments in the same building or on the same floor, not to speak of branches outside the main building. One notes damaging lack of information about what is going on outside of each little bailiwick. One hears too often that "they" are making the decision, and that "no one ever tells us what's going on."

What should be the most common and important single regular publication of any academic library with at least five staff members is a regularly issued, preferably monthly, staff bulletin. It can be an invaluable adjunct to library public relations.

It need not be as elaborate as some of those that have reached the size and consequence of being indexed in *Library Literature*. It does need to be an honest and thorough report of what is going on in the library, ranging in topics from plans for a new library building, remodeling, or annex down to a fair representation of the achievements of each department within a particular month. There is really no need to report, for example, that the leggy blonde student library assistant at the reserve desk is engaged again, but a wedding date, even among students, certainly deserves mention. The addition of a new typewriter to the catalog department's holdings hardly matters, but plans for use of a commercial or cooperative cataloging service affects the entire library and should be reported.

Include in the bulletin library and social news. Usually two or three pages per month will suffice to keep the staff informed, unified, and loyal. Send a copy of the staff bulletin each month to the news bureau and the individual to whom the head librarian reports. Every member of the library staff, including the newest student library assistant, should be on the distribution list for the library staff bulletin.

Other publications that should be included among the moderate academic library's public relations tools are reading lists, handbooks (student, faculty-graduate, or general), library-use aids (customarily one- or two-page leaflets), and bibliographies of particularly significant holdings in special fields. The reading lists and bibliographies normally should be publicized in statewide, regional, and national library media so that others may be informed of their availability.

More than any other type of library, the academic library tends to get into a rut. Academic library administrators often feel that their captive audience will use their library without inducement or advertisement. Such administrators permit the public relations of their library to become at best a series of routine announcements, cursorily prepared, desultorily issued. Then, when the library really needs its public—when the budget declines, or when the "new" annex has become old and further building is required, when the library initiates a drive for faculty status, rank, and salaries for a staff that had not achieved these essentials—it discovers that it does not have its public's backing.

It is obvious that the best public relations any institution can have is good performance. That performance would be even better if a professionally planned and executed combination of publicity, public relations, and publications let all the various publics of the academic library know just what the library is really doing. If the staff knows that its accomplishments are widely reported, it is much more likely to do a good job.

The academic library today is far too complex and costly, and far too significant for the education of its student patrons and the research and teaching needs of its faculty, to permit its use to languish. The image of the academic library can be good or bad, accurate or false, depending on its public relations.

If fewer students or faculty are using your academic library, don't fool yourself by saying "They just aren't reading any more" or "Today's students get their reading out of the bookstores" or "The faculty here is just too busy to come in." Let your patrons, actual and prospective, know what your library has to offer, and then get out of the way of the rush!

## COPY RIGHTS AND WRONGS

For many years the librarians of this country have been operating in a sort of fool's paradise, in many ways ignorant of or disregarding existing laws concerning copyright. Now, suddenly, they are beginning to worry about the implications of the new copyright laws already approved by the House of Representatives and under consideration at this time by the U.S. Senate.

### What's Behind a New Law?

There are many reasons for a new copyright law, but most of them seem to boil down to the demand by authors and publishers for the opportunity to make more money out of the publications. Under the Copyright Act of 1909—which, with a few changes, is the law which now obtains—the owner of copyright has the exclusive right "to print, reprint, publish, copy, and vend the copyrighted word." This seems pretty queer. If this were to go entirely as it says, then obviously no copy of anything that is in copyright could be printed, reprinted, published, copied, or sold without the written permission of the person or corporation which controls the copyright. We all know that every day, in Idaho libraries and elsewhere, literally hundreds of thousands, if not millions, of copies of pages, and even chapters and whole books, are made without payment of this sort to anyone. How come?

### Fair Use

One reason is that the federal courts long ago decided that there was a thing called "the right of fair use." According to a July, 1961, report of the *Register of Copyright* on the general revision of the U.S. Copyright Law, "it means that a reasonable portion of a copyrighted work may be reproduced without permission when necessary for legitimate purpose which is not competitive with the copyright owner's market for the work.[25]

This doctrine of fair use is based on the so-called Gentlemen's Agreement made in 1935 between the Joint Committee on Materials for Research and the National Association of Book Publishers.[26] This agreement, which was an attempt "to work out a code of fair practice which will protect the rights of authors and research workers," stated (in part) the following:

a library, archives office, museum, or a similar institution owning books or periodical volumes in which copyright still subsists, may make a single photographic reproduction, or reproduction of a part thereof to a scholar representing in writing he desires such reproduction. In lieu of loan of such publication or in place of such manual transcription and solely for the purposes of research; provided (1) that the person receiving it is given due notice in writing that he is not exempt from liability to the copyright proprietor for any infringement of copyright by misuse of the reproduction constituting infringement on the copyright law; (2) that such reproduction is made and furnished without profit to itself by the institution making it.

## Misuse of Copyright Materials

This agreement also stated that "the library, archives office or museum" was exempted from liability only if "library employees cautioned patrons against the misuse of copyright materials reproduced photographically." Further, it stated

it would not be fair to the author or publisher to make possible the substitution of the photostats for the purchase of a copy of the book itself either for an individual library or for any permanent collection of a public or research library. Orders for photo-copying which, by reason of their extensiveness or for any other reasons, violate this principle should not be accepted. In case of doubt as to whether the excerpt requested complies with this condition, the safe thing to do is to defer action until the owner of the copyright has approved the reproduction.

Perhaps the most interesting facet of this Gentlemen's Agreement is that it concluded with the statement that "out-of-print items should likewise be reproduced only with permission, even if the reproduction is solely for the use of the institution making it and not for sale." As we all know, there is a great tendency to say that if a book is out of print, even if it is not out of copyright, then there cannot be very much wrong with copying from it. Clearly this is not the intention of the Gentlemen's Agreement of 1935.

## ALA Reproduction Code

There have been many other attempted clarifications of "fair use" as concerns libraries, including the American Library Association's "Reproduction of Materials Code," which came out in 1941. This code, in essence, repeated the Gentlemen's Agreement, but added some precautionary measures, including the statement that "in all cases which do not clearly come under the scope of the agreement, either the scholar requiring the reproduction or the library to which the request is made should seek the permission of the copyright owner before reproducing copyright material."[27]

In the last generation, there seem to have been only two bills introduced into Congress which in any way dealt with the problems of photocopying of copyright material by libraries. The first was the so-called Thomas Bill, in 1940, which was a bill intended as a general revision of the 1909 Copyright Code. No action was taken on this bill, nor was any action taken on the Lucas Bill of 1944, which was concerned entirely with the relationship of the Library of Congress to copyright. Now comes the currently pending legislation, based on draft bills introduced in the House by Representative Celler and in the Senate by Senator John McClellan in 1964. Revised versions of these bills were introduced in 1965, and now House Bill HR 2512 has been approved by the House. Senate Bill 597 is still under consideration by Congress, and from what I heard when I was in Washington at the U.S. Office of Education in early April, it appears that the subcommittee of the Senate which is considering this law has decided to put off any action on it at least until 1969. This still does not remove its potential threat to libraries.

*Threats of Innocent Violations*

What exactly *is* the threat? The main threat is that each of us as librarians and our parent institutions may be liable, if the law as now stated is not amended in accordance with ALA proposals, to rather heavy penalties in the form of fines and even possible imprisonment for permitting, say, a coin-operated copier to be available in our libraries and to having some publisher or author become aware of the fact that, in their judgment, the "fair use" doctrine has been violated.

The bill, as passed by the House, makes a librarian in whose library "unlawful" copying is done (whether by the librarian, his staff, or a patron) liable for "costs of litigation, statutory damages up to $20,000 per infringement," and, if found guilty of having committed the offense "willfully," liable to be imprisoned for up to a year, unless he can prove in court that the "fair use" doctrine was involved.

*ALA Suggests Revision*

To avoid this, the American Library Association, meeting in Miami last winter, recommended a new Section 118 to the Copyright Revision Bill (Senate Bill 597), which would read as follows:

Notwithstanding the provisions of Section 106, it is not an infringement of copyright for a non-profit school, college, public, reference, or research library to reproduce a work, or a portion thereof, in its collection, for a user of its collection, *provided* such reproduction is not for the direct or indirect commercial advantage of the library and *provided further* that nothing herein shall excuse such user of its collection from any liability for copyright infringement that he might otherwise incur by reason of his use of such reproduction.[28]

As you see, this clearly takes the library and the librarian off the hook. Whether or not such an amendment will be approved is, of course, a matter for Congressional decision. Librarians who feel strongly about this can help by writing to their congressmen and stressing the adverse effects of the legislation as it now stands on the users of your library and yourself. The best kind of statement to our congressmen from Idaho is one which refers specifically to problems in your own library that would be created if this amendment were not approved. Naturally, since the bill is now pending in the Senate, any letters would best be sent to our senators.

## Some Representative Publishers' Claims

Just in case you do not realize how significant this pending copyright bill seems to book and magazine publishers, let me quote from a little collection I have been making in the last few months. Here are some examples of copyright notices, of the type to be found on the obverse of the title pages of books now on sale—to libraries and individuals. They are not unusual, but rather typical.

For example, Fawcett Publications, in making sure that there is no "bad" use of its books, has the following on one of them: "Conditions of Sale: This book is sold subject to the condition that it shall not, by way of trade or otherwise, be lent, be resold, hired out, or otherwise circulated without the publisher's prior consent, and without a similar condition including the condition being imposed on the subsequent purchaser."

Another publisher says (and this is probably the most common sort of copyright statement today): "All rights reserved, including the right to reproduce this book, or parts thereof, in any form except for the inclusion of brief quotations in a review."

The largest publisher in the United States, Doubleday, simply says "All rights reserved." Alfred Knopf now says: "All rights reserved under International and Pan-American Copyright Conventions."

A few years ago Harcourt, Brace, and World started to have the following statement in each of the publications: "All rights reserved. No part of this book may be reproduced in any form or by any mechanical means, including mimeograph and tape recorder, without the permission in writing from the publisher." Similarly, Macmillan now says: "All rights reserved. No part of this book may be reproduced or utilized in any form or by any means, electronic or mechanical, including photocopying, recording, or by any information storage and retrieval system, without permission in writing from the publisher." Bantam Books says: "This book may not be reproduced in whole or in part, by mimeograph or by any other means, without permission."

The one that really intrigues me is John Day Company, which says, grandiosely and eloquently: "All rights reserved. No part of this book may be reprinted, or reproduced, or utilized in any form or by any electronic, mechanical, or other means, now known or hereafter invented, including photocopying and recording, or in any information storage and retrieval system, without permission in writing by the Publisher, The John Day Company, Inc."

Horrors! I just realized that I have violated John Day's rules by quoting these few lines. I guess you will have to visit me in durance vile.

## Publisher and Librarian

Still, we should all bear in mind that this is far from being a joke. These publishers are strongly in pursuit of the American dollar, and they are a very strong and efficient lobby in supporting their views. For myself, I would wish that all publishers were like the Fund for the Republic, Inc., which states on its publications, "There are no restrictions on the use of this material." Unfortunately, not every publisher is backed by Ford Foundation money, and I have a feeling that this makes something of a difference in the attitude of the Fund for the Republic, as compared to John Day or Doubleday or Macmillan.

The question of the relationship of the new copyright law and the librarian is one that is rather difficult to discuss just now, because it is obviously far from settled. During the rest of this year, it is likely that new suggestions will be made by those on the other side; and even ALA may change its mind on what it favors in the way of protection for librarians under the proposed copyright law. No librarian wants to put publishers out of business or impoverish authors, but surely we are not going to be able to carry on our day-to-day business if we face the threat of imprisonment or large fines if we operate as we are now doing.

All of us are eager and anxious to give the fullest possible service to our patrons. We must be practical, of course, in realizing that we cannot dry up the source of book publication, namely, the publisher.

The author has invested his time and effort in the publication and is also entitled to consideration. But surely we can find what diplomats describe as a modus vivendi.

## Royalty Payments

If you want to know just how far some people involved in the publishing business can go, listen to these excerpts from the testimony of William M. Passano, president of the Williams and Wilkins Company which, as you know, is a publisher of scientific books, medical and scientific journals, and medical books. He has a solution for what he believes to be his problem in dealing with so-called stolen photocopying. His solution is this: "To us the only solution to the problem is a simple system of royalty payments with a minimum of red tape."[29] What he wants to have done is have a two cents per page tax on *all* copyrighted and copied output of libraries.

The director of marketing for Williams and Wilkins, Lyle Lodwick, in his testimony, presented a most interesting proposal. According to Lodwick, all that has to happen is that a "copying-royalty clearing house facility" should be set up, somewhat along the lines of ASCAP in the field of music, and then the individual librarians would mail in their so-called taxes on each page that is printed to the Federal government. He went so far as to suggest the Library of Congress should establish this "copying-royalty clearance" facility, "to be operational for the distribution of royalties by January 1, 1969."[30]

## Costs

When he was asked by one of the investigating senators, "Have you talked to librarians about this?" his answer was "Yes, Sir." When he was further asked, "And they say they can keep records of this at a minimum of cost?" His answer was "Well, there would be cost to it, Sir." Finally, after being pressed on this issue, he said "Whatever the setup, I think the cost of it, Sir, is minimal in terms of the problem." He saw all of this as "just another bookkeeping problem."[31]

As Lodwick went on with his proposal, it kept getting more and more complicated, and I shall not attempt to repeat the whole rather staggering conception at this time. I recommend to you the reading of pages 970-89 of Government Document Y4.J89/2C79/4/967/ pt.3. It is important reading for any librarian who in any way is involved with the copying process.

## Summary

In sum, let me recapitulate by pointing out that the new copyright bill is of immediate and great importance to all librarians, no matter what the size of the library, and no matter what type. For academic librarians particularly, especially those who now or in the near future contemplate having copying machines available to their campus community or to the general public, it is most important that you back the American Library Association amendment intended to protect you. Without responses from the grass roots, the senators will not know just how important all of this is. At the very least, let us get the two senators from Idaho strongly behind the copyright law and amendments, as recommended by the American Library Association. I hope you will keep a constant check on what is going on in this field, because it is as important to you as any single thing that is now going on in Washington, D.C.

In this brief report I have not yet even referred to the potential dangers of the new copyright law as relates to material involved with computers and computer printouts. I don't believe this is really appropriate for discussion, in terms of Idaho academic libraries as they are now equipped. But the Western Interstate Commission for Higher Education (which represents most institutions of higher education in Idaho, as well as twelve other western states), in March, 1967, strongly backed the stand of EDUCOM, the Interuniversity Communication Council, in this. EDUCOM wants renewable exemptions from copyright restrictions allowed to nonprofit educational, research, and library institutions in regard to the utilization of copyrighted works in computer operations. "They feel that S.597 as it now stands will seriously hamper educational development in this country."

The only way that you can disregard the new copyright law is if you feel that somehow the problem will just go away if you ignore it. I wish I could say this is true, but I cannot. A rather careful study of hearings over a period of a number of years and of articles and books on the subject indicates that academic librarianship in America in many respects is at a real crossroads, as concerns the possibility of providing photocopies to our patrons.

## O. P. AND ALL THAT

"Does O. P. mean Only Promises?" asked a new young student assistant working on dealer correspondence. What would you have answered?

In these many years of trying all possible avenues of approach to the interesting problem of procuring the books that college faculty members insist on the library having—the ones that are out of print—I suppose I have read and used and been confused by several thousands of secondhand dealer catalogs. They have poured into my office in all conceivable shapes and sizes, colors and formats. Patiently I have used magnifying glasses to decipher those which come in print just large enough to be read without using one of Fremont Rider's microcard readers. Soberly I have ignored the ones which feature "Curiosa," "Erotica," "Facetiae," "Unusual Book," or even "DON'T MISS THESE." Angrily I have marveled at the all too many advertisements which feature just exactly the books which we are all seeking but end a careful description of the work with the saddest of words, *Sold.*

In the first place, let us dispose of the exceptions. Only very rarely does a catalog come from an antiquarian book dealer which happens to do what any reasonable person would imagine a catalog would do. All we librarians ask is that the books be listed in alphabetical order by author (full name given), with some attempt at bibliographical fullness of entry and with an indication of the physical state of the volumes. These do not seem too impossible requirements, even in this all too imperfect world.

But what do the catalogs actually look like? O God! O Montreal!

Most common are the dealers who fancy themselves as litterateurs. Even Orison Swett Marden or Samuel Smiles never quite approaches the inspirational level of some inglorious Fourth Avenue Miltons who unfortunately have *not* remained mute. Their glee over having for sale a battered, decrepit, absolutely useless volume that no other dealer has—and that no sensible person would ever want—passeth all understanding. Their effervescent encomiums bubble over with extravagant adjectives.

Then there are the dealers who go to the other extreme. On a sheet that reaches you after being folded eight or sixteen times, they list too many books too briefly. No doubt it is worthwhile to know that they have available a book by Smith about Adams. But which Smith? Which Adams? When published? Where? By whom? Is the book an "exlibrary" copy? Is it in print? Is the binding in good condition?

Somewhere between the effusionist and the clam are, of course, the vast majority of secondhand booksellers. Their intentions are very good, I'm sure. They don't really just mail out their costly brochures to enrich the printing trades and the Post Office Department. What they want to do is, simply, to sell books.

Assuming that this is their intention, then why do they seem to the busy buyer to go out of their way to avoid anything that resembles modern merchandising methods? It is not only in catalog preparation that they fall short. There seems to be a firmly established tradition in the book trade that clearly stated requests, explaining just how invoices, statements, and similar necessary evils must be handled from the book buyer's point of view, are, in the main, to be completely ignored. It usually avails little to tell a bookseller that if the book listed in a catalog is not immediately available, he is supposed to cancel the order. No; weeks, months, even *years* later— long after you have procured the wanted item from another source— an unheralded shipment will show up in the morning's mail that means only aggravation, correspondence, and needless expense to both sides.

Yet, relationships with the bibliopole do not always drive one to aspirin. There are many wonderful moments when the book you *have* to have is the one advertised at a reasonable price and also the one that arrives, in good condition, in a few days from that indispensable—but sometimes bothersome—adjunct to library acquisition departments, the out-of-print book dealer.

## SIGHTS, SOUNDS, AND PRINT

Back in 1876, the Magic Year When the Whole Thing Began—that is, the modern library idea—the whole concept, the whole philosophy of librarianship was wrapped around reading . . . or was it? Even then there were pioneers, reformers, antiestablishment types who offered—in and from the public library—an opportunity to do things other than just read. The stereopticon (the picture slide) was widely used then—and under library auspices, too. When the motion picture film came along, there were some (not many, but *some*) librarians who felt it was their obligation to make this newest way of communication available.

Phonograph records, too, found their place in a few libraries as far back as before World War I. When the radio had its day in American life, roughly between 1920 and 1950, that generation's auditory interests were at least not completely ignored by librarians and libraries. Many libraries even had listening rooms, particularly for the portions of radio broadcasting which seemed to be more educational than entertaining. Television, of course, has been involved, in many ways, with librarians during most of its quarter-century of national prominence. Libraries the country over put on their own programs, and TV-viewing rooms certainly exist in many academic and school library situations.

But all this is not to deny that, taking all possible evidence into account, the American library is still basically, no matter whether it is called a library or an instructional materials center, a place to *read* and a place to find *reading* materials.

And what's so bad about that? Are filmstrips and films and sound tapes and videotapes and cassettes and microfilm and microfiche and disk records and all the other modern forms of conveying sights and sound *really* better ways of doing the library's job?

## McLuhanacies

Now this may seem like an easy question to answer, but on second thought, a difficulty is embodied in the fact that an answer requires a value judgment, which is bound to be based on insufficient evidence, and that any definitive answers to this would be based probably more on feelings than research. The whole communication process has been the subject of a good deal of study in the last few years; and as we all know, Marshall McLuhan, the Canadian philosopher, has been more or less the High Priest of the notion that all is new, nowadays, in the fields of communication. If one were to accept the McLuhanacies literally, one would have to accept such opinions as these: "As forms, as media, the book and the newspaper would seem to be as incompatible as any two media can be"; "Electric means of moving of information are altering our typographic culture as sharply as print modified medieval manuscript and scholastic culture"; and "the medium is the message."[32]

Let us examine these ideas as something more than mere obiter dicta. Simply because McLuhan, whose ideas have attained worldwide prominence, has said these things does not, of course, prove their truth or even their usefulness in considering the whole matter of the relationship among sight, sound, and print. It seems to me that what McLuhan has done, in general, is to take some rather dubious basic beliefs and, after accepting them as basic and truthful, used them to build up a vast structure of ideas which are far from being either true or basic, concerning our culture and its relationship to what we read, what we see, and what we hear.

He has certainly had severe criticism; Jonathan Miller, a British critic, wrote a brief biography and critique of McLuhan which pretty well covers the subject. To get an idea of the tone of the book, this is how he concludes: "Perhaps McLuhan has accomplished the greatest paradox of all, creating the possibility of truth by shocking us all with a gigantic system of lies."[33] What he is talking about, with some rhetorical flourish, is that McLuhan's chief value for most people seems to be in saying the more or less obvious, that the photograph and the telephone and radio and TV are all different kinds of media from the book, from printed matter. This is not really quite that startling an addition to the way we look at life, but it might be of value for someone who had simply ignored the obvious fact that there *are* other means of communication besides Gutenberg's 500-year-old invention.

Indeed, Miller agrees with McLuhan that "the various media *have* had their characteristic effect," but he points out further that "in acknowledging such influences there is no need to emphasize them to the exclusion of everything else."[34]

Really, I don't think it is worth our wasting any more time on the McLuhan moonbeams. They are neither illuminating, to me, nor likely to persist as a basis for consideration of communications in our time.

## Nonprint Materials

I would rather turn to a rather basic consideration of the librarian's role in dealing with the whole modern complex of possibilities for communication. If it is true that the librarian must offer to his patrons the possibility of finding out about a particular individual or idea through books, periodicals, pamphlets, newspapers, and other forms of print, why shouldn't it be true that there is an obligation to offer at least an equal enlightenment through such nonprint materials as cassettes, films, records, slides, and similar audiovisual items? This is the dilemma in which every librarian finds himself these days, because there is no question that there are many plus values to the eye-and-ear-minded rather than, to coin a phrase, to the "thought-minded," in supplying the nonprint materials. But there are a few obstacles here. The book is a very simple medium to use. It is self-contained; it requires no special machine for its reading; it requires no maintenance; it does not even use up electricity. It is, oddly enough, still the best single-packaged way of conveying thoughts and images and facts that has yet been found. Granted this, do we then denigrate the sight-and-sound materials?

I do not view this as a conflict. I rather view this as cooperation among partners—not necessarily equal (if I may exhibit my prejudices openly), but offering alternate methods of communication which can be used in unison or in combination to achieve the results we seek.

After all, what we are concerned with is the message, not the medium. I once wrote, at the height of the controversy of whether libraries should have paperbacks, some 15 or so years ago, that I didn't care whether a book was found in paper, buckram, leather, or human skin, as long as the contents within were of use to the reader. A hysterical Jewish lady from New York read this and wrote to me that I obviously had forgotten about the fact that in the Nazi concentration camps, books had actually been bound in human skin, and I was exhibiting the fact that I was callous to human suffering. All I was doing was trying to dramatize the point that the librarians of that day were being typically cautious and circumspect in avoiding any possible attraction to a new idea. Of course, times have changed; and now it seems that at least some librarians are taking the new, untried idea first and then finding out whether it was worth doing at all.

## A Good Mix

We who have been given the responsibility, as a part of our professional responsibility, of selecting materials for libraries should be acting as a link in that chain which the American Library Association long ago described as getting the right books to the right person at the right time. That statement needs to be changed so that people understand that what is meant is getting *all* types of information and entertainment and education that are available into the library and then into the hands of the person or group that needs it. The form in which the material appears is only important in the sense that it is certainly not reasonable to expect a very small library to pay the high prices that audiovisual equipment costs at the expense of not getting really needed books and periodicals and newspapers. There are always some kind of trade-offs involved in any library situation. What I am arguing for today is that we recognize the need to come to a reasonable conclusion on a good mix, one that is not related to our upbringing, or educational techniques by which we have been trained, or other nonrelated points. If the material is best made available to our patrons in the form of videocassettes, and if we can afford the new cassettes and players which can use cassettes, then let's get them. Let's not do as one library I heard of recently, which used some of its federal money a few years ago to buy three reader-printers and then wrote to the library in a nearby town and asked for microfilms so they could check whether the reader-printers worked.

One of the simplest and most direct statements I had ever read about the book and its relationship to other means of communication is the one that was printed in the American Library Association volume entitled *The Future of General Adult Books and Reading in America.* It said, "the book is the most compact and efficient device for the storage and retrieval of information of ideas that the world has yet discovered."[35] This is a rather sweeping statement, but one that is pretty hard to controvert. Now the mere fact that it is the best does not necessarily mean that it is *always* going to be the best, or that there aren't others which, in special cases, might not be better. On the whole, the book is certainly better; but of course, there are situations in which information retrieval systems, programmed learning, viewing, all sorts of different ways of getting information are appreciably better than the book could possibly be.

But then, again, you can't push an information retrieval system against a door to keep it from slamming, can you?

Seriously, we are running into a situation as librarians where we really have to face up to the excesses to which both the ultraconservatives and the ultrainnovationists are heading. If you were to read some of the advocates of the so-called media center, you would think this was a brand-new idea that never existed before the word *media* was invented. As I have already pointed out, the various media have been in and used by libraries and library patrons for a great many years. Changing the traditional name of the library to media center or any other of an assorted gallimaufry of specialized titles that have been used all over the country in the recent past does not change the fact. A library is a library is a library; or maybe it isn't! If it provides the materials that its patrons need, I guess that it is a library; if it doesn't, I don't really know what it is.

## The Future

The predictions that have been made by some of our soothsayers about the future are quite radical and surprising, and, I have no doubt, several will come true. But I remember very clearly that in the 1940s the film was supposed to take over. I remember that in the 1950s the programmed teaching machine was going to take over. I remember that in the 1960s they began talking of cassettes and videocassettes being on the verge of breaking out. Now, in the 1970s, the videocassettes and still other possible technological improvements on various machines we already have will no doubt become the new item to talk about, the hot item that everyone needs to know and use.

But I really hesitate to make anything like absolute predictions about communications. If I were forced to come to some conclusions about the relative values of materials that are available for seeing and hearing and reading, I would have to say that the book has had a longer period of time to develop than the new contenders, and necessarily it not only is better but should be better. What will happen with the comparatively infant developments along the lines of television and information retrieval remains to be seen.

We, as librarians, should no more be censorious of the forms in which library materials come than of the contents of the materials. We cannot very well defend the Library Bill of Rights and at the same time look down our noses at any particular form in which the information or education or recreation happens to come. Our responsibility is to know about *all* of the different varieties that we can learn about, to have some kind of standards by which to select them, and to try our best to get the budgets with which to afford them. All of this may sound unduly optimistic, particularly in Idaho in 1973. With our restricted budgets, present and anticipated, and with the blow that we have just received these past few months from the disappearance of federal funds, it is not too likely we are going to flourish as the green bay tree and have money to throw around. But that doesn't mean that new forms should be ignored and scoffed at.

Let me conclude with a totally undocumented, nonresearched series of observations which may explain my perhaps by now fairly evident bias toward *print*. Along with most librarians of my generation, I do my share of televiewing, of radio listening, of motion-picture film watching, of theater going, of lecture attending. But when I want to study something, I still go to reading material to do so. In my judgment, whether you were born in 1950—and so have spent, on the average, five hours or more of each and every day of your life since you were four or five years old watching television—or, like me, you were born in 1915—and so average at least two hours per day of reading—you still cannot derive your considered judgments on matters of intellectual importance from anything else than the book.

I, for one, promise that the next time I have an urge to buy a book, I will call up Book Readers Anonymous and get someone to convince me that I really have to kick the habit and get turned on by something much more psychedelic or cacophonous or, maybe, even imaginative. After all, could any book possibly manage to match "Hee-Haw"?

## THE LIBRARY PATRON'S BILL OF RIGHTS

All librarians are familiar with and understandably proud of the noble set of ideals we have, through the American Library Association, set up for ourselves in the Library Bill of Rights. This is a document which is definitely not hyperbole and rhetoric; it has been converted into positive, helpful action on many, many occasions and throughout our nation.

But what about the person who uses the library? What are his rights? Perhaps it would be overpretentious to call what I shall have to say an expression of a "bill of rights." The Library Bill of Rights does deal with some of the deeper issues of our time, indeed of all time, which affect libraries and patrons alike—such matters as censorship, the right of peaceable assemblage, and freedom of access to knowledge.

What I am concerned with are the rights of the library patron to such simple but often overlooked rights as the right to ordinary courtesy, the right to equal treatment with others, the right to ask questions about anything under the sun and expect help in finding answers, and the right to reasonable peace and quiet in the library without the requirement of deathly silence. "Patrons," as Sarah Wallace wrote some years ago, "are people," and they deserve to be treated as such. They are also taxpayers and, for most of us, our salary payers. If we forget that we are servants, not masters, of the people, we deserve to be no longer given the opportunity to serve.

There are other rights that patrons have. They have the right to express disapproval as well as commendation of our doings as librarians. They have the right to expect a polite hearing of their grievances as well as their plaudits, if any. They deserve the same treatment from us that we like to get when we are the askers and must get answers from others. They are entitled to reasonable consideration of their problems, whether we consider them great or small.

It may seem very trivial to you, for example, when a patron complains of the way the shades on a particular window are not pulled, so that the sun's rays keep him from comfortable reading. After all, we want the shades to look even from outside, to improve the external appearance of our building! But what good is an aesthetically pleasing, geometrically aligned row of shades if our patron leaves in high dudgeon, and we have not only lost a reader but perhaps gained an enemy when bond-issue time comes around?

Let us consider some particular rights that are most fundamental. The patron has the right to come into the library at all times and find someone there ready, willing, and able to give him service. Idaho public libraries are open short enough hours, as we all know, and every one of those hours deserves equal staffing. If your building is open, it should have the best available person on hand to give the best kind of service possible. In my opinion, if you cannot staff in this fashion, you should not keep the building open those particular hours when the staffing is impossible.

The library patron deserves to have as much comfort in seating and reading space and good light and appropriate heating and ventilation as possible. It makes a mockery of a library building to have it there with not enough heat in the winter, too much in the summer, the kind of lighting that makes bifocal users wince, and old, battered splintery chairs, and too few and too small tables. The library should be as comfortable and inviting for reading as one's own living room, if not more so.

Now, let me return to the patron's right to reasonable peace and quiet in the library, to which I referred very briefly a few moments ago. Sometimes I have a feeling that library staff members all think they wear the ring of Gyges, described in Platonic legend as a brazen ring which rendered King Gyges invisible. Brazen some librarians are, and blatant and loud, too. We "shush" our patrons but answer the telephone in a public area in a loud tone, speak to our friends in normal speaking voices, and, in general, act as though we were both invisible and acoustically insulated.

One of the rights of a library patron that is often given only lip service is his right to variety. I am not referring to that item in the Library Bill of Rights which states that "there should be the fullest possible practicable provision of material presenting all points of view concerning the problems and issues of our times, international, national, and local; and books and other reading material of sound factual authority should not be proscribed or removed from library shelves because of partisan or doctrinal disapproval." This is, of course, fundamental. What I mean by the right to variety is that even if we are speaking of books which are not on supposedly controversial issues, a patron is entitled to some choice. Get two books on how to train a dog; have several volumes on garden planning. The unique volume, which is usually out, is not really of much value to your library patron.

I know that budgets are slim; but any library, in my opinion, is better off with six different titles on a subject than with six copies of one book on that subject, in almost every case. Don't overload on one author, or one topic, or one publishing house. Give the patron not only the right to choose, but enough reading materials to give him an opportunity to exercise that right.

We librarians all too often become so involved in our daily outlines that we forget the great importance of communication. Library language, as we all know, tends to become as jargonish as the language of any other profession. Your patron knows little and cares less about "L. C." or "D. D." and would much rather listen to straight, simple talk than to abbreviation-laden, esoteric gobbledygook that is literally nonunderstandable to him. Save the library gibberish for your library articles, if you must use it. Let's leave the pseudo-scientific pedagoguery to our friends the documentalists; librarians should concentrate on getting ideas and facts across in the plainest, most direct way possible.

Another pet peeve of mine is the chastely decorated library whose virginal walls are never desecrated by such mundane things as directional signs. Tell your patron where to go—and I don't mean what that sounds like. Seriously, I feel that every library has the obligation to guide its patrons by signs, directory boards, or handbooks to its various sections. Any library which is housed in more than one small room has different places for different kinds of materials. Your patrons should not have to ask you for ordinary directions. Both your time and theirs can be saved by use of sufficient and clearly understandable signs.

I suppose that among the fundamental library rights is the patron's right to a useful card catalog. The card catalog that is filled with circular, boomeranging cross-references, that is not kept up to date, that has less than the minimum of appropriate subject cards, that lacks useful guide cards, that is arranged so that only a master filer could find in just what order the cards are filed—any card catalog that is like this deserves what it gets, disuse by patrons. And if patrons don't use your catalog, why bother to maintain it at all? Take away the case, use the backs of the cards for scraps, and reconcile yourself to a library that is operating on much less than one cylinder.

Now, to return to perhaps more vital considerations in this discussion of the Library Patron's Bill of Rights. I am sure the American Library Association will never, in its august majesty, either consider or approve the list which follows; but here, for what it is worth, is my suggested Library Patron's Bill of Rights. Those which I thought needed elucidation or elaboration have been given due notice. The rest, I believe, are self-explanatory.

## The Library Patron's Bill of Rights

1. Every library patron is entitled to courtesy and respect so far as his own conduct justifies such consideration.
2. Every library patron is entitled to reasonable peace and quiet in the library, without unnecessary distractions by other patrons or by library staff members.
3. Every library patron is entitled to his say on library book selection and also entitled to responsive and clearly explanatory statements from the librarian on library book selection policy.
4. Every library patron is entitled to the best seating, ventilation, heating, and general decor possible in the library.
5. Every library patron is entitled to as nearly as possible equal quality of service any time that the library is open to the public.
6. Every library patron is entitled to a choice of books, whether on major topics or by major authors, or on minor topics or by minor authors, so far as space and funds permit.
7. Every library patron is entitled to a logically arranged, easily accessible collection, with simple directions to guide him in its use.
8. Every library patron is entitled to a card catalog which is suitable to the type of collection cataloged and to the type of patron making use of it.
9. Every library patron is entitled to library service that goes beyond the routine and trivial to satisfy as far as possible the ever-changing needs of the individuals and groups that make up the library's community.

In that wonderful pamphlet recently issued by the U.S. Office of Education, "The Public Library: For Lifelong Learning," we are told that "every man, every woman, every child can make the exciting discovery that use of the public library leads to individual growth—

whether that use is for information, for fun, or for inspiration."[36] Let us librarians not be the ones to stand as barriers between people and that "exciting discovery" of which these writers speak. Let us observe the Library Bill of Rights *and* the Library Patron's Bill of Rights. The results just might amaze you.

## NOTES

1. Charles H. Haskins, *The Rise of Universities* (New York: Holt, 1923), p. 52.
2. Ibid., p. 53.
3. C. E. Sayle, "King's Hall Library," *Cambridge Antiquarian Society Proceedings*, vol. 23, n.s. vol. 17 (1920-21), pp. 54-75.
4. William Mather Lewis, *From a College Platform* (New York: Dial Press, 1932), p. 229.
5. *A History of Columbia College on Morningside*, p. 16.
6. Carl White, *Changing Patterns of Scholarship and the Future of Research Libraries* (Philadelphia: University of Pennsylvania Press, 1951), p. 58.
7. Ordway Tead, *Trustees, Teachers, Students* (Salt Lake City: University of Utah Press, 1951), pp. 31-32.
8. B. L. Johnson, ed., *The Librarian and the Teacher in General Education* (Chicago: American Library Association, 1948), p. 21.
9. L. R. Wilson et al., *The Library in College Instruction* (New York: H. W. Wilson, 1951), pp. 283-308.
10. George A. Works, *College and University Library Problems* (Chicago: American Library Association, 1927), p. 2.
11. Ibid., p. 5.
12. Ibid., p. 67.
13. Ibid., p. 76.
14. Ibid., pp. 33-104.
15. S. C. Roberts, *British Universities* (London: Collins, 1947), p. 44.
16. Johnson, *The Librarian and the Teacher in General Education*, p. 5.
17. Ibid.
18. Ibid., p. 7.
19. Ibid.
20. Ibid., pp. 21-22.
21. Ibid., p. 34.
22. LeRoy Merritt, "Notes of Merritt," *Library Journal* (November, 1959), p. 3548.

23. This article first appeared, in somewhat modified form, as "Displays for the Academic Library," *Idaho Librarian* (October, 1970), pp. 135-38.

24. Good sources for ascertaining such anniversaries, whether of people or events, are the following: A. Black and C. Black, *Writers and Artists Year Book* (Boston: The Writer, annual); M. Stanford Mirkin, *What Happened When* (New York: Washburn, 1966); *Chases' Calendar of Annual Events* (Flint, Mich.: Apple Tree Press, annual); Neville Williams, *Chronology of the Modern World* (New York: McKay, 1968); and Miriam A. Deford, *Who Was When?* 2nd ed. (New York: Wilson, 1950).

25. U.S., Congress, House, Judiciary Committee, *Copyright Law Revision: Report of the Register of Copyright on the General Revision of the Copyright Law,* 87th cong., 1st sess. (Washington, D.C.: Government Printing Office, 1961).

26. "The Gentlemen's Agreement of 1935," *Reprography and Copyright Law,* ed. Lowell H. Hattery and George P. Bush (Washington, D.C.: American Institute of Biological Libraries, 1964), pp. 157-58.

27. "Reproduction of Materials Code," *ALA Bulletin* (February, 1941), p. 84.

28. "Midwinter in Bal Harbour," *ALA Bulletin* (March, 1968), p. 276; as corrected in *ALA Washington Newsletter* (April 8, 1968), p. 2.

29. U.S., Congress, Senate, Committee on Judiciary, Subcommittee on Patents, Trademarks, and Copyrights, *Hearings . . . Copyright Law Revision* (Washington, D.C.: Government Printing Office, 1967), pp. 974-76.

30. Ibid., pp. 977-89.

31. Ibid.

32. Marshall McLuhan, *Understanding Media* (New York: McGraw Hill, 1964), pp. 9, 171.

33. Jonathan Miller, *McLuhan* (London: Fontana/Collins, 1971), p. 132.

34. Ibid., p. 120.

35. Peter S. Jenison and Robert N. Sheridan, eds., *The Future of General Adult Books and Reading in America* (Chicago: American Library Association, 1970), p. *vii*.

36. Helen E. Wessels and Rose Vainstein, "The Public Library: For Lifelong Learning," OE-15025 (Washington, D.C.: U.S. Office of Education, 1961).

# 4 ASSOCIATION

LIBRARY ASSOCIATIONS:
THEIR HISTORY AND INFLUENCE

About fifty years ago W. Somerset Maugham, in a notable novel, *Of Human Bondage,* included a fable which has some direct bearing on the topic of the history and influence of library associations. A young prince in an Eastern land was suddenly thrust into the leadership of his country by the unexpected death of his father. The new king called in his council of wise men, some seventy or eighty brilliant souls, and asked them to prepare for him a history of the world, so that he would be in a position to lead his state among the nations in an appropriate manner. Some years later he called in the head of the council, which by then had shrunk to perhaps fifty or sixty individuals, and said, "Where is that history?" The answer was, "Sire, we are bringing it in today"; and in staggered the fifty or sixty men, each bearing a giant tome. The king indignantly said to the chairman of the council, "Off with you. I don't have time to read all that stuff. Bring me a condensed version, and I want it soon." A few more years passed. Again the council chairman was called in. This time some ten or twenty men came in with twenty large volumes. The king was almost beside himself with rage, and said "I don't care how long it takes you, I want a condensed version. I can't read all this stuff!" Off the sages went. Finally the king, now in his later years, called in the old, weary head of the council and said, "How about that history that I've been after you for these many years?" And the chairman replied, "Sire, there are no longer any members of the council left except me, and I can give you a history of the world right now." "Well, what is it? What is it?" The answer came, "Man was born; he suffered; he died."

This is a rather lugubrious beginning for a paper intended to be informative and perhaps even inspirational. The point is that most library associations in existence are past the first stage and into the second. Those that are not in the second stage have gone all the way.

What have been the birth pangs; what have been the struggles; indeed, what might even be the cause of dissolution of library associations? There is neither time for nor interest in every statistical detail of the rise and fall of various library associations. The most significant library association in the United States, the American Library Association, is now heading toward its 100th year, which it hopes to celebrate in 1976. The first state association, the New York State Library Association, was founded in 1890. The same year saw the founding of state library associations in Ohio, New Hampshire, Massachusetts, and New Jersey, succeeded by five more in 1891— Connecticut, Maine, Michigan, Minnesota, and Wisconsin. Within ten years, a total of twenty-eight state organizations had been established; and at present, there are library associations in fifty states, the District of Columbia, and Puerto Rico.[1] In Canada, the history is similar.[2] The Canadian Library Council was established in the 1930s, and the present Canadian Library Association began its existence in June, 1946. There are presently in Canada one regional and six provincial library associations. In the United States, there are five regional associations and either thirty-six or twenty national library associations, depending upon whether the various divisions of ALA are considered separate national associations or parts of ALA. There are, in addition, many local and library-related associations, which are not germane to this discussion.

The historical considerations of the development of library associations are well chronicled in the January, 1955, issue of *Library Trends* and elsewhere in library literature. It seems, therefore, more important to stress the responsibility and influence of library associations than their history.

## Birth of Library Associations

The birth of library associations, in America at least, came about through the influence of a man not entirely unknown to librarians. Although some library historians pay respect to the first national library conference ever held, in New York City on September 15, 1853, it was clearly not until 1876 that, through the efforts of Melvil Dewey, the American Library Association was established.

As usual with Dewey, he was not content with a single achievement along a particular line. He attempted and as usual succeeded in more and more activities and achievements.[3] In June, 1890, Dewey wrote in *Library Journal,* urging "ALA members in each state which is not yet organized to take immediate steps toward a beginning" of local library associations. He said that "as soon as there are five or more interested library workers in any state, they ought to put their names together in a state association, which will grow with the growth of public sentiment and keep its place on the state's roll of honor." It is interesting to note that the dates of the organization of the first ten state library associations were 1890 and 1891, since it was only June, 1890, when Dewey first pointed out in *Library Journal* that "the time has come when we need local associations to carry on the rapidly developing modern library work."

The objectives of the first state library association were:

The stimulation of interest in New York by addresses, articles in the press, circulation of printed material etc.; the securing of the fullest possible cooperation with ALA in promoting general library interests; the promotion among New York libraries of the exchange of duplicates, inter-library loans and other forms of cooperation; securing the adequate library legislation; and the enrolling of all interested in library development.[4]

These are still the concerns of state and regional associations today, though certainly this is not all. Associations are involved in a wide variety of activities, and as might be expected, individual associations may vary their particular interests from year to year or from decade to decade.

## Activities

It would be impossible to list all of the activities in which library associations engage. These range from furnishing scholarships to prospective librarians to active lobbying in state legislatures (a very common form of activity), to leadership in such areas as the promotion of intellectual freedom (as in California, Wisconsin, New Jersey, and many other states), to the promotion of library publications. The impressive publication programs of such national groups as the American Library Association are well known. Perhaps not as well known are the publications of such an association as the Pacific Northwest Library Association, which has been responsible for a rather large group of worthwhile library publications.[5]

At the instigation of the association, and with its cooperation, Charles W. Smith edited *Pacific Northwest Americana: A Checklist of Books and Pamphlets Relating to the History of the Pacific Northwest,* which was published by the H. W. Wilson Company in 1921. A list of *Special Collections in Libraries in the Pacific Northwest* was put together by the same Charles Smith in 1927, this volume published by the University of Washington Press. John Van Male put out a much more detailed version of this, entitled *Resources of Pacific Northwest Libraries: A Survey of Facilities for Study and Research,* some 404 pages in length, in 1943. The third edition of Smith's magnum opus, *Pacific Northwest Americana,* appeared, as revised and extended by Isabel Mayhew, in 1950. A *Who's Who Among Pacific Northwest Authors* was edited by Hazel E. Mills and published, with the cooperation of the Pacific Northwest Library Association Reference Section, in 1957.[6]

Perhaps most significant of all, a four-volume set under the general rubric *Pacific Northwest Library Association Library Development Project Reports,* edited by Professor Martin Kroll and written by him and various members of the Pacific Northwest Library Association, was issued in 1961. This covered such topics as *The Public Libraries of the Pacific Northwest, Elementary and Secondary School Libraries of the Pacific Northwest,* and *Libraries and Librarians of the Pacific Northwest.* No region in the United States has been so thoroughly studied from a library standpoint as the Pacific Northwest, due entirely to the efforts of leaders in the Pacific Northwest Library Association. The four volumes are a monument to the work of the individuals and to the association, which was responsible for obtaining the Ford Foundation grant to finance the project and to publish the results. The Pacific Northwest Library Association, incidentally, was the progenitor of the *Subscription Books Bulletin,* now published by ALA. The *Subscription Books Bulletin* was first published by PNLA, in two series, from 1917 to 1929.

In other areas of activity, the leaders in library associations are well aware of their responsibilities in influencing legislation, both on the state and national level. Without the cooperation of the state library associations, the ALA Washington office could never have become a reality. The office is still heavily supported by state associations. Without this office, librarians would never have attained the dream of the 1930s, that at least $100 million in federal money should be appropriated to promote library services throughout the country.

*Influence*

It is difficult to define the actual and potential influence of library associations, particularly if this involves prognostications for the future. There are state associations which serve mainly as mouthpieces for state libraries and even for state legislatures. There are other library associations which merely serve the purpose of providing opportunities for like-minded people to get together and exchange experiences. This is certainly a worthwhile purpose, but hardly justification for the amount of time and trouble that usually goes into the work of library associations.

In 1952, Alice Bryan wrote *The Public Librarian* as part of the Public Library Inquiry. The volume includes the only study I know of giving a broad sampling of the opinions of librarians in regard to professional associations. Bryan found that, as of 1947, "about a third of the professional librarians in the inquiry sample attended meetings of their state and local library associations, 18 percent attended the annual meeting of the ALA, and 14 percent went to one or more meetings of regional organizations." She found that "the median length of time spent by the group as a whole, including traveling time, in attending meetings of library and other professional associations during 1947 was less than half a day." She found that "those librarians who attended meetings averaged 2.2 days for the year."[7]

Most significant about the Bryan study is that, when asked which organizations had in the preceding years been very helpful in contributing to the effectiveness of their library work, "not more than one-eighth of the librarians found membership in any of the organizations listed very helpful professionally."[8] The group as a whole found the American Library Association and community library organizations the most helpful. Bryan summarizes: "As librarians in service, the group in the basic sample read their professional literature, join their professional associations, pay dues, attend meetings, and serve on committees in a moderate degree."[9] She summarizes further: "For the most part they do not have the sense of conscious professional or personal benefit from professional association membership or activities that prevails in more closely organized and regulated professions."[10]

Perhaps this has implications for what the influence of library associations *could* be. Every kind of association for professional librarians, ranging from that which serves the interests of like-minded librarians in a neighborhood of a large city to the mammoth American Library Association, could well have *more* influence than is presently the case. Oliver Garceau, in his Public Library Inquiry volume, said that "serving as they do in widely scattered units, each with an inherently limited potential, librarians have a peculiar need for association as a means of organizing their ideas, their aspirations, and their influence beyond the scope of the individual unit."[11] He admits that librarians have "sought not only the obvious goals of pressure politics but also the self-respect and status of a professional group, with the development of standards, the interpretation of function in terms of the ideology of the community, and the beginnings of a code of ethics that are concomitants of professionalism."[12] He asserts that librarians have used the American Library Association "as a central service agency on an unusually broad front to complement the work of the local library units."[13] But he claims (and although this was eighteen years ago, it is probably as true today) that the American Library Association is hamstrung by the "wide range of education and intellectual perspective . . . among practicing librarians."[14] He grants that the American Library Association has at least a facade of democracy. Garceau questions, as I do, whether the American Library Association would not be of immeasurably more benefit to its members if state and regional chapters were more than merely groups from which council members are chosen. How true is it that the American Library Association, as it is presently functioning, reflects the will and the desires of its members?

## The American Library Association

It might be worthwhile to recapitulate some of the points in a recent article in the *ALA Bulletin.*[15]

The American Library Association has developed into a very important organization, not only for libraries and librarians, but also for many other groups and individuals. Recommendations made by ALA are given high priority in decisions made by governmental groups on every level of our society:

We are involved in the work of groups which decide how thin or thick a catalog card should be, how lasting a book page, how high is up, and how low is down. We help guide the school and college training of thousands, the building of multi-million dollars worth of libraries. Even, to some extent, the ALA influences authors and publishers in the writing of books.[18]

ALA sends representatives throughout the world to participate in the activities and conferences of hundreds of organizations and institutions, both library and nonlibrary, from Switzerland to Hong Kong.

All this rehearsal of how ALA is flexing its muscles, now that it has reached the ripe age of 90, is preliminary to a fervent plea that we act our age. We cannot afford, it seems to me, to behave as though we were a group of self-sufficient, self-motivated individuals. We are beginning to be a Colossus of sorts; the pigmy days are long over.[17]

This indictment of ALA is documented in some detail in the article, and there is no need to repeat the strictures therein contained. The point here is that *most* associations—and certainly library associations are no exception—once they become large in membership and settled in their ways, have a tendency to "let George do it." To a great extent, ALA is following the pattern of ignoring what the grass-roots membership wants, not with any malice aforethought, but simply because it is in the nature of very large organizations to treat the people at the bottom of the hierarchy as less knowledgeable than those at the top, with increasingly less need to be consulted.

Another point made in the article is that, like large corporations, ALA is falling into the pattern of "a long period of slow growth and development, a relatively short period of reformulation both of basic structure, underlying beliefs, a short period of rapid expansion, and a period of varying length of time of relative dominance."[18] At the time of the Public Library Inquiry, Garceau pointed out that less than half of our profession are members of ALA.[19] This compares with such professional organizations as the American Medical Association or the American Bar Association very much to our discredit. Certainly, in the ensuing 20 years this situation has changed, but not very much. When one considers that ALA includes about 5,000 institutions in its membership of some 31,000, along with trustees and other individuals who cannot by any stretch of the imagination be called "professional," it gives great cause to question whether ALA truly represents professional librarianship in America. Certainly its English counterpart, the Library Association of Great Britain, *does* represent professional librarianship in that country. Garceau, incidentally, had another comment which may be of significance here. He referred to ALA in 1949 as "a maze of overlapping, ill-defined groups, some very active and eager, some rather confused." Is this too unlike the situation which *now* exists?

To return to the comparison of ALA with the growth of a business corporation, "ALA has had the long period, the relatively short period, and the short period."[20] In other words, ALA has gone through the slow growth and development, the relatively short period of "reformulation both of basic structure and underlying belief," and is now in the process of what may well be a "short period of rapid expansion." Now the question is, how long will the period of "varying lengths of time of relative dominance" last? Already we see signs of great difficulties within the association, as well as strong opposition from the ruling hierarchy against any massive changes.

There is nothing sacrosanct, it need be pointed out, about the form of organization of any group whatsoever. Of course, it is also true that there is nothing inevitable about massive change. But when signs appear of what seem almost irreconcilable tensions, perhaps the organization should be looked into. This would be a salutary measure for any type of library organization, if it is to maintain influence and justify its past history.

Referring again to the Maugham fable, if it is true that eventually ALA will suffer and die, the inevitable end need not be within any foreseeable future; and the suffering can certainly be minimized. It is merely necessary to understand that such things do happen. Should ALA die within the present era, out of its ashes may come a phoenix of even greater value than its predecessor. This is not intended as a

Cassandra-like prediction of the complete collapse of ALA. Unlike the sayings of Cassandra, it is an attempt to look constructively at what might well develop if those in authority fail to see the peril and take corrective measures.

This description of ALA as it exists today is not necessarily the story of other library associations. But it could be. It is the responsibility of the membership of any association to look into its history and future prospects and to weigh, deliberately and thoughtfully, whether it is in a situation which overlooks possibilities for improvement in the future in being too much concerned for what seem to be the urgent demands of the present.

Alexis de Tocqueville, a century ago, described the American system of voluntary association as "a dangerous freedom." In his comprehensive and acutely aware volume bearing that title, Bradford Smith stressed that Americans must continue "to live active lives of service," if democracy is to survive.[21] Librarians can do no less, however "dangerous" this freedom becomes.

## INTELLECTUAL FREEDOM, CENSORSHIP, AND LIBRARY ASSOCIATIONS

The work of national library associations, particularly that of the American Library Association, in terms of positive action to protect the freedom to read and constant vigilance against censorship, is well known to all librarians. The widely publicized Freedom to Read statement, active participation in significant court cases as amicus curiae, the publication of books, articles, and booklists—these are among the most significant and socially useful activities of the American Library Association.

On the state level, too little is known of the activity or utter lack of activity of a fairly large number of state library associations in this regard. It is not expected that a state library association continually tilt its lance at windmills merely to prove its support of the Library Bill of Rights and the Freedom to Read statement. Yet all state library associations should be somewhat active in these areas. There is never a real truce in the continuing battle between Mrs. Grundy and those who really believe and insist upon their right to practice the

First Freedom, the Freedom to Read. A list of suggested anticensorship activities for state library associations might include:

1. Urging librarians of public, school, and academic libraries to promulgate and practice the concepts of the Library Bill of Rights and the ALS Freedom to Read statement.
2. Acting as a clearinghouse and friend-in-need for librarians and libraries involved in censorship cases.
3. Involvement as needed, by public statement and even by direct action, when institutions, individuals, libraries, and librarians are confronted with censorship difficulties. If the principle of the freedom to read is denied to book stores and magazine shops, the next victim will be libraries.
4. Making available the help of those best qualified within each state to assist in dealing with unnecessary censorship legislation, as it is introduced in state legislatures. If it seems that a particular censorship law will inevitably pass, the state library association should determine that such a law is valid (in accordance with state and federal constitutions) and workable (at least insofar as libraries are concerned).
5. Acting as an arsenal of experience and reliable advice for all who need assistance in defending the freedom to read.
6. Strongly backing the activities of the American Library Association, providing all possible state library association resources and personnel, as needed, in anticensorship fights.

There is never a time when the library association can afford to disregard a censorship situation. When state library associations fail to assume a position of leadership, their very indifference assists the forces of darkness and denial of truth. The long and difficult history of defense of the individual's freedom to read proves that it cannot be left to the national associations to do battle in these areas. Within each state library association there should be an officially designated and publicized committee on intellectual freedom, even if this is only a one-man committee to serve as a watchdog. Censorship sometimes crops up suddenly, permitting little time for setting up ad hoc committees. Men and women who are capable of grappling with the problems of censorship and who have a strong background of such knowledge and experience are available in every state. Such librarians, and nonlibrarians, should be alerted to serve whenever the need arises.

The Intellectual Freedom Committee of the American Library Association, as well as the administration and the membership of ALA, can be called upon when time permits. Often, however, cases must be dealt with effectively and immediately and on a local or state level. This is the responsibility of the state library association.

Several state library associations have been helpful in the censorship battle by issuing "freedom to read kits" or other compilations of material on the subject. In spite of the value of such information, however, nothing replaces the articulate individual or the convincing group when assistance is suddenly required. It is not sufficient to rely upon information in the pages of pamphlets, books, or periodicals except where those in need of such information are aware of its existence and know how to use it.

Each state library association should be prepared to face a serious case of censorship on a local or statewide basis. The state library association must be constantly alert, always ready to do all that can be done to thwart censorship. The state library association which abdicates its share of responsibility for maintaining the freedom to read is no longer a leader in any phase of librarianship. The core of librarianship is the active advocacy and defense of the freedom to read.

## WHAT THE INDIVIDUAL MEANS TO ALA

ALA, at first glance, seems complex, tradition-shackled, and autocratic. Look beneath the surface, and see ALA for what it really is: a group of dedicated individuals, inspired by a long and honorable tradition, performing tasks that must be done to keep the library profession and library service in their proper places in today's society, and working together in democratically organized rapport.

No organization could long survive, let alone grow to the position of national and international stature held by ALA, without a decent respect for each member's opinions and needs. The army librarian out on a lonely base in frozen Thule, the visiting library consultant in sunbaked Istanbul, the bookmobile librarian in the high mountain passes of Idaho, the busy children's librarian in a crowded city branch library—all are united in a common cause by the American Library Association.

Within its broad scope are every type and variety of librarian and library-minded person. By the terms of its constitution, only two requirements exist for membership; interest in library service and librarianship, and payment of dues. There are no restrictions because of race or creed or political belief or educational background. Each member is a member because he is interested in advancing the broad concept of providing books and information to people. Whatever contributes to this is ALA's interest.

The individual member furnishes the know-how and adds to the numerical strength of the organization. Well over half of ALA's income comes from yearly dues paid by individual members. In their thousands, the membership of ALA bring knowledge and power to bear on the mutually significant problems of their profession. The individual member is the source and the strength of all ALA planning and action; without him, ALA could not exist.

## A CONSTITUTIONAL CRISIS IN THE ALA?

The American Library Association is becoming a prestigious organization. In a few years it has gone from less than 20,000 to its present 31,000 plus, including nearly 5,000 institutional members and affiliated or member associations. The reorganization of ALA, which went into effect in 1957, was a result of the Management Survey, made by Cresap, McCormick, and Paget during 1954-1955. The survey came about as a belated result of the Fourth Activities Committee, under the chairmanship of Ralph R. Shaw, which reported on December 15, 1948, in a report which covered twenty-seven pages of the January, 1949, *ALA Bulletin,* including two major sections and a total of eighty recommendations.

One of the matters singled out by this committee as being the reason for its coming into existence at all was that there was "confusion in management of the Association by its double-headed organization of Council and Executive Board, each responsible directly to the Membership." A great many of the members had the opinion that the Fourth Activities Report and the Management Survey might result in simplification of the ALA structure.

Instead, seventeen years after the Fourth Activities Report and more than a decade after the Management Survey, we have a complex of suborganizations almost impossible to explicate. Only recently this was increased (after less than ten minutes of public deliberation) by the addition of another division, that of Information Sciences and Automation.

Certainly, it is obvious that the Fourth Activities Report and the Management Survey have resulted in a much more complicated and less of a grass-roots organization than was contemplated. At each of our midwinter and annual meetings, there are literally hundreds and hundreds of official and unofficial meetings of the various ALA groups.

We have grown so large that our treasurer this year informed us that the $1 million "borrowed" from the ALA Endowment Funds just a few years ago to help pay for the new ALA building was already returned, in the light of profits earned upon ALA investments because of the booming economy.

In view of the ALA's size, age, and international importance, how is it that we still continue our old practice of assigning vital responsibilities to but a very few? At the recent Chicago Council meetings, a number of committees of Council reported—and the duplication of names was both obvious and ominous. Out of a council of several hundred members, of whom perhaps three-fourths were present, surely it cannot be true that pretty much the same people *must* serve on committee after committee after committee. We are beginning to hark back to the 1946 era, when only a grass-roots revolt of indignant, democracy-seeking members broke up the tight little "in" circle holding and allocating power.

Scott Buchanan has recently written, with deep concern, about "the corporate veils and legal fiction under which corporations carry on their vital private governments."[22] The ALA is a corporation, and its "veils and . . . fiction" exist, whether we like it or not.

One of the "fictions" of ALA is that institutions which become ALA members do not have any power, under our setup. At the 1966 midwinter conference, a member of the Clapp Committee, which was formed for the purpose of considering the matter of qualifications for institutional membership, told us that the only real purpose of having institutional members within ALA was to raise money for the American Library Association. He deprecated the value of such memberships also, as being but the occasion for duplicate copies of ALA publications coming into the institution and as having the empty honor of being included in the *ALA Directory*.

Somehow I got the impression that it was practically a favor on the part of any institution to join ALA, that it was all show on one side and charity on the other, that the association, not the member institution, was the real gainer from such affiliation.

I disagree with the premise of this, because along with institutional membership goes also the vote, and a block of nearly 5,000 votes is quite important in deciding policy, since policy is decided by the Executive Board and Council, and ALA institutional members have the right to vote for both. But even if we were to grant the point that institutional membership is a very empty honor, perhaps it might be considered at this time that there should be a major change in ALA makeup. Let us continue affiliations of associations which may find benefits in such affiliations, and out of whose affiliation ALA may benefit, but let us, effective January 1, 1968, discontinue all institutional memberships.

One of the dangers of authority under diffused responsibility is the unhappily too frequent recurrence of events happening which are obviously not the result of reasonable, logical deliberation by all of those affected. We have had the following sequence of events recently in ALA: A resolution proposed by an individual member was passed by the membership present at a regular association convention meeting. The resolution was also backed by an eight to four majority of the ALA Executive Board. An ad hoc Committee of Council, picked by the president of ALA, proposed scrapping the resolution, and by a very large majority of the ALA Council, the resolution, although it was backed by both a representative group of the total membership and by the Executive Board, was scrapped. Please bear in mind that these Council members were put in office in several different ways: (1) ex officio, (2) as a courtesy, (3) by direct vote of the ALA members, (4) as chapter representatives. (Chapter representatives are voted on by entire chapters, even though a majority of the membership of a chapter need not be members of ALA.)

R. W. Boyden, in the book cited earlier, says, "the center of the . . . corporation, however, appears not to be people, but rather something called the 'firm,' or the 'going concern.'"[23] This is about what seems to have happened with the ALA.

Further in his comments, R. W. Boyden points out that the expansion of the corporation seems to follow the formula: "a long period of slow growth and development, a relatively short period of reformulation both of basic structure and underlying belief, a short period of rapid expansion, and a period of varying lengths of time of relative dominance." ALA has had the long period, the relatively short period, and the short period. Now, it would appear, we are going through the period of "relative dominance," but how long will it last if our present method of organization continues?

Boyden points out that "various symptoms of crisis can be observed in ... corporations. One such symptom is simple failure to do the job for which the particular corporate type was designed." Another such symptom, he states, is "the accumulation of unused wealth." Still another is "a failure of beliefs." Then, he says, there are a set of "political symptoms which are even more alarming—a tendency to grow in a size on a scale which has no connection with the original function and to add miscellaneous other activities to justify the size." (This has been elsewhere referred to as Parkinson's Law.) He stresses that along with this comes "a tendency to develop a command structure within the corporation and a tendency to favor political despotism outside it." This certainly sounds very unsavory, and something which we should avoid.

Boyden offers some constructive suggestions for improving the corporation, which might be most salutary for ALA to consider. He states that "the center of my suggestion is that corporations be reconstituted as made of people." He says that when the associational element is really lost sight of, it leads to "fuzziness of purpose, an incredible metaphysics ... and meaningless growth." Does this sound familiar, in the light of some of the factual statements made above?

Mark Twain once said, "It is by the goodness of God that in our country we have these unspeakably precious things: freedom of speech, freedom of conscience, and the prudence never to practice either." I am happy to state that I lack the prudence recommended by the cynical Mark Twain. It is my hope that a great many other individual ALA members will echo my sentiments and do what is needed to once more make ALA what it should be—a free, untrammeled association of library-minded individuals, dedicated to the cause of better and wider library service for all who need it.

In my mind, nothing but a Fifth Activities Committee, standing aside from the Council and the Executive Board, and including representatives of the dissident as well as the always faithfully agreeing groups and individuals in ALA, will suffice to create a new ALA, in time for our Hundredth Anniversary, of which our entire profession may be truly proud.

## ATTITUDES ON SEGREGATION: HOW ALA COMPARES WITH OTHER PRO-FESSIONAL ASSOCIATIONS

*How do the actions and statements of ALA on the segregation issue compare with those of other national professional associations— in breadth, force, and achievements?*

*This was the question Eli Oboler set out to answer as a result of correspondence published in the* ALA Bulletin, *July-August issue, pp. 608-9. He wrote to the executive secretaries of 22 national professional associations and received replies from all but one of them.*

*Of the 21 associations which submitted answers, only ten had made any official statements or taken any kind of action in this matter, and the bulk of Mr. Oboler's article is devoted to reproducing, almost in their entirety, the statements of these associations.*

*It is clear from an examination of these statements that ALA compares most favorably with the majority of other associations both in what it has done and what it proposes to do in the near future. As Mr. Oboler says towards the end of his article: "ALA seems to be well above the middle range of the professional associations in its statements of policy, as well as in some of the actions already taken and now under consideration."*

*We are glad that this should be so because we believe that librarians and the association which represents them should be leaders rather than followers of society, and that their statements should be in the forefront of current liberal thinking on all important social issues.*

*That ALA ranks so well in this matter with the leading professional groups should not, however, be cause for self-satisfaction. Much remains to be done, and we should do all that* can *be done.*

*Only one or two of the statements which are reproduced in Mr.*

*Oboler's article suggest policies or actions which might yet be adopted by ALA. We would draw particular attention to the statements from the American Association of University Professors, the American Nurses' Association, and the National Association of Social Workers.*

*Each of these three, and the NASW resolutions and statement of goals in particular, contains very positive elements which should be seriously considered for future implementation by ALA.—ed.*

Before presenting the statements by the various professional associations, I would like to quote from a statement made by I. D. Haskew, dean of the College of Education and vice-president for Developmental Services of the University of Texas. Dr. Haskew wrote—and I believe this to be as appropriately said for ALA as for NEA—

American society today is dependent, to a degree seldom realized, upon the actions, interactions, and counteractions of organized professionals. To the professions, important trusteeships have been assigned; much of the effectiveness with which individual members of a profession discharge that trusteeship is dependent upon the action of the professional organizations to which they all belong. . . . all of us have a tremendous stake in what organized professionals leave undone, what they try to do, and how well they do what they have decided upon.[24]

This statement seemed to me a setting prelude to what follows.

The letter that I wrote to the twenty-two association executive secretaries was as follows:

I am making a study of current professional attitudes toward segregation and integration of American Negroes. I would appreciate your sending me a brief statement of what, if any, action or statement has been made by your organization since 1954 concerning the problem of segregation in the United States. If your organization has taken no official action or made no official statement, I would appreciate having this information also. If, by any chance, there is a published document of which you have a copy available, which conveys your association's attitude on this question, I would appreciate your sending me a copy. If such a statement has been published but you have no copy available, please send me a bibliographic reference to it.

Of the twenty-one associations which replied, eleven indicated that they had taken no official action in this matter. They were: the American Association of Engineers, the American Bankers Association, the American Bar Association, the American Institute of Certified Public Accountants, the American Institute of Electrical Engineers, the American Institute of Industrial Engineers, the American Society for Microbiology, the American Society of Civil Engineers, the Botanical Society of America, the National Society of Professional Engineers, and the National Association of Retail Druggists.

Six of these stated specifically, however, that they had Negro members, and the American Society of Civil Engineers mentioned a "duly instituted Student Chapter of ASCE [which] has been in operation at Howard University since 1951." The American Institute of Electrical Engineers, however, said: "This subject is completely outside our scope. This organization knows nothing of race, color, etc.—never gives it a thought."

The ten national professional associations which indicated that some statement had been made or action taken gave rather more lengthy replies. Here is what they said:

## American Chemical Society

I could comply with your request simply by saying that the American Chemical Society "has taken no official action or made no official statement" on the matter of segregation. Yet that would create an erroneous impression of our attitudes. It is difficult to make clear why we have no such statement and yet at the same time declare that the organization does not practice segregation.

Many Negroes are members of the American Chemical Society; I can give no statistics because such information is not pertinent to our work. Our only concern is in regard to competence in the field of chemistry. Some of our Negro members are personal friends of mine; a number hold or have held positions of responsibility in this organization. I think it is these very people who best understand why the Society has not passed resolutions. Such statements have been considered by our Council which in our governing scheme is equivalent to a House of Representatives. Debate has been free and frank and only once or twice, heated. Yet all such motions have been tabled and many persons in favor of desegregation have voted for such action.

We have held meetings in segregated areas and through advance arrangements and gentle persuasion have had privileges not available to those who come in "off the street." Not always have we been as successful as expected; sometimes we have been more so. It seems generally recognized that what we have accomplished represents some progress without a fight and progress perhaps greater than achieved by those who demand all or nothing.

I would summarize ACS attitude in this way: I believe the organization as a whole is opposed to segregation, but it has passed no resolutions nor do I think it will do so (although it is risky to predict). I believe we have been more successful in pushing back the boundaries in those areas where integration exists than have the individuals, groups, or organizations who have been militant and blatant in their method of approach. However, this is only a personal opinion.

## American Dental Association

Membership in the American Dental Association is established at the local level. The only membership that is granted at the national level on a direct basis is that of dentists in the federal dental services and membership for dental students.

In its report to the 1960 House of Delegates the Board of Trustees of the American Dental Association made the following request:

The American Dental Association and its constituent and component societies are established to make the benefits of professional organization available to members of the profession. The Board of Trustees, therefore, requests that the constituent and component societies study their by- laws with the view to insuring that there are no provisions which restrict membership on the basis of race, creed, or color.

Since this request was made in October 1960, a majority of the Association's constituent and component societies have responded stating their positions. No societies have reported any bylaw provisions which restrict membership on the basis of either race, creed, or color.

*American Association of University Professors*

"I am enclosing verifaxed copies of the resolutions concerning segregation, which have been passed by the Annual Meetings of this Association beginning with 1956, inclusive of those passed by the Forty-Seventh Annual Meeting on April 21-22, 1961 in Boston." The 1961 resolution referred to is as follows:

The Forty-Seventh Annual Meeting of the American Association of University Professors reaffirms the resolutions of previous Annual Meetings with reference to racial segregation in education. It calls attention to the pressures in a substantial number of academic communities in the South, which have resulted in the suppression of ordinary freedom of utterance for faculty members and students on matters of race relations. This suppression is having a pernicious effect upon higher education, especially because of the reluctance of qualified scholars to become and remain members of faculties in communities where it exists. The problems that beset all of us because of segregation will remain unresolved until it becomes possible for individuals and groups to express their beliefs in the moral rightness as well as the legal necessity of racial desegregation and to work for its accomplishment without fear of reprisal. We affirm the duty of this Association, its chapters, and regional units to direct unstinted efforts, in this important matter, towards the attainment of full academic freedom.

The association letter continued:

Also enclosed are a reprint of a report entitled *Academic Freedom and Tenure: Allen University and Benedict College* from the Spring 1960 *AAUP Bulletin,* and a copy of the Spring 1958 *AAUP Bulletin,* which contains, among others, reports on Alabama Polytechnic Institute (now Auburn University) and Texas Technological College. On the basis of these reports the Association voted to place the administrations of these institutions upon its list of Censured Administrations. . . .

The enclosed reprints of *Segregation and the Professor* and *Implementation of Supreme Court's Decision on Racial Segregation in Public Education* may be useful to you as well.

## The American Institute of Architects

... The American Institute of Architects has taken no official position since 1954 on the explicit issue of segregation of American Negroes.

However, by virtue of having Negroes in its membership, the problem has arisen in connection with its conventions and certain actions have been taken in relation thereto. Enclosed you will find a copy of our "Memo" of January 19, 1959, which comments on the problem as affecting our New Orleans convention and the position of the Institute at that time.

In November 1959 the Board of Directors passed the following resolution: "Resolved, That facilities be selected for national conventions which do not restrict any members of the AIA in the exercise of their membership rights as defined in the latest Bylaws and related documents."

Essentially the same wording is carried in "AIA Policy Statements," 1960 edition, p. 19.

## American Mathematical Society

"The attitude of this organization is that we will not hold meetings when any of the facilities used by us at the meetings are segregated."

## American Psychological Association

... let me quote the relevant section from our Rules of Council: The Annual Convention of the Association shall be held only in those cities which meet the following conditions:

a. Racial discrimination shall not be imposed by state law or local ordinance and shall not be commonly practiced in the use of public transportation, public buildings, public recreational facilities, major hotels and restaurants.

b. The Association shall have been given the assurance by those in charge of convention arrangements for the host city that discrimination will not be encountered in hotels, restaurants, and such other facilities as are explicitly employed by the Convention.

It shall be the responsibility of the Convention Manager to present evidence to the Board of Directors that

these conditions will be met before any binding com-
mitment is made to a given city.

This statement was adopted first in September 1958, by our
Council of Representatives, as official Association policy. In September 1960, all past actions of the Council were incorporated into a
formal document, known as Rules of Council.

## American Medical Association

In June 1934, the House of Delegates of the American Medical
Association adopted the following resolution:

Resolved, That the American Medical Association in
annual session assembled condemns the persecution of
any individual on account of race or religion by any state
or under any flag.

This resolution has never been rescinded and stands as the official
AMA policy to the present time. We have not taken any stand with
regard to the American Negro, but the above policy may be general-
ized to include any racial group.

## American Nurses' Association, Inc.

We are pleased to be able to report positively to your inquiry
regarding progress towards integration within the profession of
nursing.

You will be interested to know that the American Nurses' Association is the only professional organization that has an inter-group
relations office unit and staff member working full-time in the area
of meeting the needs of minority groups. The staff member serves as
a consultant to the other programs at the national headquarters, as
well as to state organizations; as guide to a national committee
occupied with intergroup problems; and as liaison with allied organizations in this field (Urban League, National Association of Intergroup Relations Officials, National Council of Christians and Jews,
National Catholic Interracial Council, etc.).

We are enclosing copies of statements of the American Nurses'
Association, reflecting our policies and practice. . . .

The relevant statements are as follows:

(From "The Code of Professional Nurses," adopted 1950, revised 1960)

2. The nurse provides services based on human need with respect for human dignity, unrestricted by considerations of nationality, race, creed, color or status.

(American Nurses' Association Platform . . . 1960-62.)

11. Encourage full participation of all members in association activities and work to eliminate discrimination in employment and educational opportunities for nurses.

In addition, the ANA has issued a statement, "ANA Policies and Principles on Intergroup Relations," which includes the following "Policies Adopted by the ANA Board of Directors":

1. That there be no discrimination as to race, creed, or color in accommodations obtained for ANA meetings. Adopted, ANA Board, January, 1948.

2. That there be no discrimination as to race, creed, color or sex in making appointments to the headquarters staff. Revised and reiterated, ANA Board, January, 1955.

3. That there be no discrimination as to race, creed, color or sex in appointing members of ANA committees. Revised and reiterated, ANA Board, January, 1955.

4. That the Economic Security Unit be asked to give special attention to the need for opening employment opportunities in the broad sense—employment, promotion and retention, each on the basis of merit—to Negro and other minority group nurses. Adopted, ANA Board, 1955.

5. That the ANA Committees on Legislation support those bills on civil rights issues, introduced in Congress and the legislatures, which will have a favorable effect on nurses, nursing and health, and speak in opposition to any bills which would have an adverse effect. Adopted, ANA Board, April, 1954.

6. That there be no discrimination as to race, creed, color or sex in the administration of registries and counseling and placement services; and that registries and counseling and placement services inform patients and agencies which use their services of this policy. Revised and reiterated, ANA Board, January, 1955.

7. That the Mary Mahoney Award be perpetuated to give impetus to the efforts of individuals or groups of persons toward the ultimate achievement of nursing goals based on sound principles of human relations. Adopted, ANA Board, April, 1954.

8. That ANA action on federal and state legislation involving civil

rights and affecting nurses, nursing and health be in accord with the following statement of principles: *Statement of Principles re: Legislation Involving Civil Rights*

a. A favorable climate of federal and state law is essential to the achievement of the long-term goals of the Intergroup Relations program of the American Nurses' Association. The Association should promote and support legislation designed to provide a climate in which discriminatory practices affecting nurses, nursing and health may be eliminated.

b. All qualified applicants, regardless of race, creed, color or national origin, should have the same opportunities for sound educational preparation for nursing. Tax funds for the support of nursing education should not be used to initiate or perpetuate discriminatory practices.

c. Legal restrictions to the full utilization of nursing personnel which are based on race should be eliminated.

d. Legal restrictions to the unsegregated use of public accommodations should also be eliminated.

e. Health and welfare programs supported by tax funds should promote and protect the physical, mental and social well being of all citizens regardless of race, creed, color or national origin.

## National Association of Social Workers, Inc.

To answer your request for a statement of positions taken by this association in regard to integration, I am sending you the section on civil rights and liberties from the association's *Goals of Public Social Policy*, and also three resolutions adopted at Delegate Assembly of the association in Chicago last October.

These positions are not all confined to segregation and integration of American "Negroes" but should fit in to the material you are gathering.

Included among the recommendations in *Goals of Public Social Policy* are:

1. *Integration.* Social agencies and schools of social work which by fiat or tradition institute or continue practices of racial discrimination which are inconsistent with the spirit of the Supreme Court decision should seek to comply with the law and the spirit of that decision.

2. *Financing Public Services.* All forms of governmental aid and support for public services, benefits, or facilities should be conditioned upon their availability to all eligible persons without discrimination on the basis of race, national or regional background, sex, religion or other beliefs of affiliations, or on the basis of any moral judgments by the government not sanctioned by law.

3. *Antidiscrimination Laws.* The right of all, regardless of race, religion, national or regional origin, sex, or political and economic beliefs to employment which is based on training, competency, and skill must be protected by law. Many states and cities have fair employment practice laws. Federal regulations make similar requirements of employers filling defense and other federal contracts. This right should be extended throughout all areas of employment, governmental and voluntary.

Further, the right of all to access and use of public accommodations and services and to public facilities must be assured by law.

4. *Equal Treatment Before the Law.* All persons who are otherwise qualified should have the right to vote, to hold office, to serve on juries, and to receive both the protection of the law and a fair trial according to democratic principles of jurisprudence, if accused of crime. Where state and local machinery fails to protect the constitutional rights of any person, or state and local governments use their power or tax funds to contravene constitutional rights, the federal government should take steps to correct these abuses.

5. *Co-ordination and Leadership.* To provide a systematic and critical review of social needs and public policy and a continuous appraisal of the status of civil rights a permanent federal Commission on Civil Rights with powers of subpoena should be established.

Two of the three resolutions to which the NASW letter referred concerned public school desegregation. The first, which concerned federal action, read in part as follows:

. . . BE IT RESOLVED that the NASW endorse and urge action on measures to:

1. Empower the Attorney General to file civil injunction suits in cases involving denials of the right to equal education opportunity, in order that Negro or other children may not be denied their rights.

2. Require every school district affected by the Supreme Court's School Desegregation Decision to submit a plan for compliance no later than the close of the 1961-62 school term, and to authorize the

Department of HEW to develop a desegregation plan, enforceable in the Courts, for any school district which fails to submit its own plan within the time prescribed.

3. Deny federal funds and subsidies to any school district which refuses to admit students because of their race, religion, color or national origin.

The second resolution was concerned with the question of NASW chapter action in relation to public school desegregation. In part, this read:

... WHEREAS, the chapters of the National Association are located by geographic areas and therefore are in a position to reflect local conditions.

THEREFORE BE IT RESOLVED that NASW supports Chapters in cities and localities where there is de facto segregation in public schools in taking appropriate steps to break down segregation and develop integrated schools.

BE IT FURTHER RESOLVED that NASW supports Chapters, in States where laws have been passed to block school integration, make all possible efforts, through programs of discussion and education, to develop acceptance of the need to comply with the Supreme Court decision. . . .

*National Education Association*

... The official position of the NEA is set forth in the platform and in the resolutions adopted annually by the Representative Assembly. I am enclosing a copy of their resolutions adopted last year and would call your attention to the one on desegregation on page 60. Similar resolutions have been adopted since 1954. They will be found in the volume of *Addresses and Proceedings* and in the *NEA Handbook*.

Here is the 1960 resolution on "Desegregation in the Public Schools":

The National Education Association believes that integration of all groups in our public schools is an evolving process which concerns every state and territory in our nation.

The Association urges that all citizens approach the matter of desegregation in the public schools with the spirit of fairness, good will, and respect for law which has always been an outstanding characteristic of the American People. It is the conviction of the Association that all problems of desegregation in our schools are capable of solution at the state and local levels by citizens of intelligence, saneness and reasonableness working together in the interests of national unity for the common good of all.

The Association commends the communities which have handled their problems regarding desegregation in such a manner as to assume their responsibility to maintain the public schools and their obligation to recognize the political and professional rights of teachers. It commends also the officers and directors of the National Education Association for their vigorous and effective support of state and local education associations when the professional rights and status of teachers were unfairly menaced and for having prepared and published the forthcoming National Education Association report, *Studies of Educational Problems Involved in School Integration.*

The 1961 Atlantic City NEA Conference approved a resolution affirming "continued support" of the 1954 Supreme Court decision on public school desegregation. It voted down, by a narrow margin, an amendment to this resolution that would have requested the NEA officers to "plan and initiate action" to back up the United States Supreme Court decision.

You will have noted that there is a wide range of attitudes among the various professional associations. Some have done nothing, a few have done a great deal; but in general, ALA seems to be well above the middle range of the professional associations in its statements of policy, as well as in some of the actions already taken and now under consideration.

There is no need, obviously, for those of us in the library profession to feel that we are not in the mainstream of national professional thinking. Although it has taken time and effort, clearly what we have done and what is now under discussion and study deserves commendation rather than censure. Nevertheless, the American Library Association and its members cannot sit back and say, "We have done enough and can rest on our labors." In November 1954, Grace Marr, assistant executive secretary of the Intergroup Relations unit of the American Nurses' Association, wrote an editorial for the *American Journal of Nursing* which said several things which could well bear study by our association. The editorial stated (in part):

The professions, because of the leadership they exert in society and because of the unique qualifications which their members hold, have a special obligation to provide leadership in the integration of members of all racial and religious groups in our society. The professions are committed to serve mankind; they function with public approval and should merit the faith which the public places in them. It has been members of the professions who have uncovered scientific knowledge which shows the fallacies in the theories in which traditional discriminatory customs and practices have rested.

Professional people are experienced in human relations matters, their practice is influenced by all civil rights legislation, and they enjoy social prestige which leads persons in other occupations to emulate them. As a result, their leadership is especially needed in efforts to attain integration. If they simply await the passage or the enforcement of laws which favor integration, or await the development of a community's readiness to attain integration, they sacrifice the opportunity to provide leadership in the enactment of sound civil rights legislation and in the general practice of sound human relations. . . .

Discriminatory practices affecting members of racial or religious minority groups in any profession become the problems of the entire profession, not of just the minority group involved. A profession concerned with fulfilling its moral obligations cannot afford to close its eyes to discriminatory practices within it or affecting it. It cannot refuse to give objective consideration to these practices and the means for eliminating them. Such a profession seeks, rather, to learn what discriminatory practices there are, if any, and how they can be eliminated. . . .

Providing leadership in any controversial situation is difficult at best. It is far simpler to find reasons for taking no action on problems that give rise to controversy than to appraise them objectively and to develop methods to solve them. The challenges appear formidable in some parts of the country and relatively minor in others. But this may be misleading. Action on controversial issues, whether it is constructive or not, is contagious. A profession cannot afford to ignore the challenges in integration; a unit of that profession cannot afford to consider itself immune from their effects.


Far more important than whether we catalog according to one code or another, whether we offer four years of training or five years for our practitioners, or whether we use machines or people to perform certain library tasks is whether, on a vital national issue

which directly affects libraries all over the nation, we as a profession
are willing to stand up and be counted and assume the responsibilities
which every profession worthy of the name should assume. I, for
one, feel that ALA has proceeded with undue "deliberate speed" and
really needs to increase the pace and force of its activities, let alone
its policy statements, concerning freedom of access to libraries in the
United States.

## THE CASE FOR ALA REGIONAL
## ANNUAL CONFERENCES

More and more, there are indications that the American Library
Association is earnestly endeavoring to make itself more truly democratic. At the Kansas City meeting, the decision was reached no
longer to permit voting privileges to institutional, rather than personal, members. Membership meetings, year after year, seem to indicate a good deal of grass-roots feeling that occasionally even vetoes or
transcends the actions of the ALA Council. Younger members of
ALA are asking for—and getting, in many cases—much more adequate
association.

On one level, however, there has been a great deal of foot-dragging
during the past twenty years. Although it was pretty widely accepted
that the 1949 regional conferences—held over a period of more than
three months in seven different locations—were quite successful, not
since then have such regional conferences been held or even discussed
to any great extent. The major reason for this, so far as I know, has
been the opposition of ALA headquarters to the "inconvenience"
involved in holding meetings over such a long period of time and in
so many places. I base this assumption on some private conversations
with various members of headquarters during the intervening years
and also on some rather interesting tangential indications, which may
or may not be significant.

For example, the recorded list of regional conferences, the "official" list published in the *ALA Membership Directory,* although it
includes attendance figures for every convention since 1876, lists the
dates and places of the regional conferences in 1949 but does not
give any attendance. The notation says: "Attendance not recorded."
It is just possible that this kind of evidence is similar to the famous
"Chops and Tomata Sauce" evidence in the trial of Bardell against

Pickwick. (Non-Dickensians may refer to chapter 34 of the *Pickwick Papers* for details.)

At any rate, there certainly have been nothing but "normal" conferences since the 1949 experiment. If one major indication of total interest and concern with the American Library Association is the percentage of membership attending, it might be worthwhile to examine the figures from 1950 through 1967, the latest date for which accurate figures are available. Here is Table 1, which presents the official figures for attendance, total membership, and percentage of total membership attending.

TABLE 1

| Location | Year | Attendance | Membership | Percentage of Membership Attending |
|----------|------|------------|------------|------------------------------------|
| Cleveland | 1950 | 3,436 | 19,689 | 17.5 |
| Chicago | 1951 | 3,612 | 19,701 | 18.3 |
| New York | 1952 | 5,212 | 18,925 | 27.5 |
| Los Angeles | 1953 | 3,258 | 19,551 | 16.6 |
| Minneapolis | 1954 | 3,230 | 20,177 | 11.5 |
| Philadelphia | 1955 | 4,412 | 20,293 | 21.7 |
| Miami Beach | 1956 | 2,866 | 20,285 | 14.3 |
| Kansas City, Missouri | 1957 | 2,953 | 20,326 | 12.8 |
| San Francisco | 1958 | 4,400 | 21,716 | 20.3 |
| Washington, D.C. | 1959 | 5,346 | 23,230 | 23.0 |
| Montreal, Que., Canada | 1960 | 4,648 | 24,690 | 18.8 |
| Cleveland | 1961 | 4,757 | 25,860 | 14.5 |
| Miami Beach | 1962 | 3,527 | 24,879 | 14.2 |
| Chicago | 1963 | 5,753 | 25,502 | 22.6 |
| St. Louis | 1964 | 4,623 | 26,015 | 22.1 |
| Detroit | 1965 | 5,818 | 27,526 | 21.1 |
| New York | 1966 | 9,342 | 31,885 | 29.3 |
| San Francisco | 1967 | 8,116 | 35,289 | 22.9 |
| Kansas City, Missouri | 1968 | 6,500 (est.) | 40,000 (est.) | 16.3 (est.) |

A second chart (Table 2) indicates the "run" of percentages and attendance, indicating that the mean for the past nineteen years was 18.8 percent of the total membership and that this represents 4,648 persons attending. But for the past five years, the average percentage has been up to over 25 percent of the membership, and the attendance has been nearly 7,500. It may also be pertinent to point out that of the nineteen meetings listed, twelve were held east of the Mississippi and seven west.

TABLE 2

**Range of ALA Conference Attendance**
1949-1968

| Percentage of Membership | Attendance |
|:---:|:---:|
| 29.3 | 9,342 |
| 27.5 | 8,116 |
| 23.0 | 6,500 |
| 22.9 | 5,818 |
| 22.6 | 5,753 |
| 21.7 | 5,346 |
| 21.1 | 5,212 |
| 20.3 | 4,757 |
| 18.8 | 4,648 |
| 18.3 | 4,623 |
| 17.8 | 4,412 |
| 17.5 | 4,400 |
| 17.1 | 3,612 |
| 16.6 | 3,436 |
| 14.5 | 3,527 |
| 14.3 | 3,258 |
| 14.2 | 3,230 |
| 12.8 | 2,953 |
| 11.5 | 2,866 |

I do not happen to have available the current figures for residence of the various personal members of ALA, but it is obviously true that any time ALA holds a conference in the East, it is likely that there will be larger attendance than one held in the West. There has been one notable recent exception to this, and this was the particular meeting which had the fourth highest percentage of attendance of any of the nineteen being discussed, the one at San Francisco. Of importance in this connection is the statement by the Executive Board of ALA at its 1968 annual meeting in Kansas City, that "the Association is now limited to eight cities because of its needs, these being Atlantic City, Chicago, Las Vegas, Miami Beach, New York, Dallas, Denver, and San Francisco, with some question remaining about the latter three.[25] It should also be pointed out that a rather definitely planned for, although not finally scheduled, conference in Seattle in 1970 was shifted to a different site, because of the belief of the conference manager that Seattle could not house ALA members adequately. Also, at Kansas City, "upon recommendation of the conference manager, the Board canceled plans for the 1972 ALA Conference in Boston, and a new site is being sought. Growing conference attendance and programs make it clear that facilities in Boston are not adequate."[26]

What this boils down to is that we seem to have a situation where there is an increasing percentage of ALA members who would *like* to go to ALA meetings and a decreasing number of cities which could possibly house large enough conferences.

My recommendation, simply put, is that the Executive Board of ALA seriously consider planning toward either quinquennial or decennial regional conferences. Surely the conservatively estimated doubling of "normal" attendance which regional conferences would bring more than justifies the undoubtedly rigorous schedule which would have to be maintained that particular year by the officers of the association and the headquarters staff members involved. There would certainly be some problems about getting cooperation from the exhibitors. All of these seem trivial in comparison to achieving what must be more and more active participation by its membership in the work of the association. Meetings held at the five (or possibly eight) places listed above cannot possibly bring in the grass-roots participation which regional meetings would be bound to achieve.

I personally plump for regional ALA conferences every five years, starting as soon as possible, since it is perfectly clear that despite the rather lengthy advanced planning which we know must be done in relation to sites for conferences, it is always possible to change these until definite contracts are signed. Why *not* regional conferences in 1972? A new site has to be decided upon, anyway, for that year. The centennial ALA conference, as we all know, had long been planned for Philadelphia in 1976; now we are told Philadelphia will not be that year's site.[27] Why not, then, another regional series of conferences in 1976 or 1977? And the tradition, once begun as such, could more or less easily be maintained from then on. The yeasty risings and stirrings of the younger members and dissident members and uninvolved members of ALA, being felt in so many ways and indicated in so many ways throughout the last few years, should not have to develop into a revolt before action is taken.

After the one (and only) series of regional conferences, the ones held in 1949, there was not one, but two, committees established by the Executive Board to evaluate the regional conferences. To the best of my knowledge, no reports of these committees were ever published. It would be interesting to know what they recommended and even more interesting to discuss this matter as early as possible, preferably at the midwinter meeting, and see how the membership feels about it.

I have a hunch that, for once in my rather checkered ALA career, I am likely to find rather a great preponderance of opinion in favor of something which I support, even at the beginning of what I hope will be far from a futile campaign to help make ALA into what we all would like it to be, a truly democratic and participative association.

## NOTES

1. John S. Richards, "State and Regional Library Associations," *Library Trends* (January, 1955), pp. 319-29.

2. Gerhard R. Lomer, "The Background of the Canadian Library Association," *Canadian Library* (May, 1964), pp. 299-302.

3. Richards, "State and Regional Library Associations."

4. Ibid.

5. I have some personal knowledge of this work both as a member of the PNLA for the past eighteen years or so and as the former editor of its regular publication, the *PNLA Quarterly*.

6. Ruth Hale Gershevsky, *PNLA 1909-1959: A Chronological Summary of Fifty Eventful Years* (Seattle: Pacific Northwest Library Association, 1959), p. 41.

7. Alice I. Bryan, *The Public Librarian* (New York: Columbia University Press, 1952), p. 137.

8. Ibid.

9. Ibid.

10. Ibid.

11. Oliver Garceau, *The Public Library in the Political Process* (New York: Columbia University Press, 1949), p. 152.

12. Ibid.

13. Ibid.

14. Eli M. Oboler, "A Constitutional Crisis in the ALA?" *ALA Bulletin* (April, 1966), pp. 384-86.

15. Ibid.

16. Ibid.

17. Ibid.

18. R. W. Boyden, "The Breakdown of Corporations," in *The Corporation Take-Over,* ed. Andrew Hacker (Garden City, N.Y.: Anchor Books, 1965), p. 52.

19. Garceau, *The Public Library in the Political Process,* p. 153.

20. Oboler, "A Constitutional Crisis in the ALA?"

21. Bradford Smith, *A Dangerous Freedom* (New York: Lippincott, 1954).

22. Scott Buchanan, "The Corporation and the Republic," in *The Corporation Take-Over,* ed. Andrew Hacker (Garden City, N.Y.: Anchor Books, 1965), pp. 17-39.

23. Boyden, "The Breakdown of Corporations," p. 50.

24. I. D. Haskew, "Dimensions of Professional Readership," *NEA Journal* (February, 1961), pp. 25-26.

25. *ALA Bulletin* (July-August, 1968), p. 842.

26. Ibid.

27. *ALA Bulletin* (October, 1968), p. 1137, n. 5.

# 5 OBFUSCATION

## LIBRARY STATISTICS:
## WHY, HOW, AND MAYBE

Library statistics, like library rules, seem to be a problem to all libraries and librarians, whether college, public, school, or special. The unpleasant but unavoidable necessity of reporting our activities regularly to some higher authority has impelled some librarians to almost incredible feats of rationalization for keeping records otherwise not even remotely justified. Other librarians seem driven to a Spartan simplicity of record keeping that offers only minimum, if any, usefulness.

Perhaps most common of all statistics is the record of circulation. Some libraries circulate books for seven days, some for two weeks, some for a month; some permit renewals, others do not; some keep track of so-called table circulation, others don't. Yet this farrago of "facts" about circulation is proudly promulgated as if these differing and varied records really mean something. Indeed, very often—if the figures warrant it—circulation statistics are used as a public relations device to show the library's public and its administration that use of the library has gone up 10 percent or 20 percent or 30 percent or whatever.

Rarely do these circulation statistics take into account variances in lengths of loan periods or renewal policies or even such outside factors as significant rises or declines in the population of the public for the library, changes in travel patterns occasioned by highway or street changes, or even unusual weather conditions. Any or all of these little items might very well have affected circulation figures much more than internal library policies. Still, year after year circulation figures are published, with hardly any insight or explanation as to their direct meaning.

And what is the "direct meaning" or potential usefulness of statistics? They are useful, it seems to me, either for reporting or for internal planning. When properly selected and maintained, library statistics serve as a historical record for significant progress, or lack of it, in library holdings or services. They are a report of the past to help better the future—or at least *good* statistics could serve this purpose.

Favorable comment on the value of statistics could well be out-weighed by as much or more unfavorable comment. All too often statistics are simply "busy work," the keeping of interminable records of inconsequential details. Indeed, sometimes they are deliberately maintained as a device to prove a moot point, which is really not at all predicated on the facts coming out of the statistics.

One of the most frequent crimes of the statistics addict is the tendency to compare unlike or very little alike situations in different libraries. What earthly good is it to find out, for example, that your library repairs twice as many or half as many books as the library in the next town or the neighboring state? Just what are "repairs" in your library—spit-and-string jobs or a thoroughgoing overhauling in-volving recasing, rebinding, and so on? How much rebinding work does one library send to a commercial bindery, as compared to another? Which library buys two or more copies of a very popular book and so saves wear and tear on individual volumes? A myriad of problems arise the minute one begins to look behind the so-called comparison and tries to find out the true facts of any part of the operation of any library.

The statistics of the libraries of Idaho are as varied as the libraries themselves, but there are some general patterns ascertainable. By state law, public libraries must report certain statistics to the state library board. College libraries report both to their own institutions and to the U.S. Office of Education, Library Branch. School libraries, if one may judge from the recently announced Idaho State Department of Education School Library Standards, need practically no statistics. Under the section of the standards dealing with "essential elements of library records," no reference is made to attendance, or circulation, or any other statistics of use or growth. Supposedly, then, no records of this type need be kept for reporting purposes.

The most recent U.S. requirements for college and university libraries, as reported in "Library Statistics of Colleges and Uni-versities, 1959-60, Part 1: Institutional Data," ask for detailed data on the size and rate of growth of the library collection, on size and type of library staffs, on library expenditures, and on relevant institutional data. Also, salaries of full-time personnel are requested. Interestingly enough, *no* circulation or attendance figures were requested, although this type of statistic is maintained, I believe, by almost every college and university library. A much more detailed report is issued for the state-supported institutions of higher education in Idaho, as part of the regular biennial report of each institution.

The most detailed statistical requirements for any type of library in Idaho are those listed in the State Code for Public Libraries. Idaho state law (Idaho Code 33-2606) requires for public libraries' annual reports to the State Library Board to show, among other things, "the number of books and periodicals on hand, and the number added by purchase, gift or otherwise during the year, the number lost or missing, the number of books loaned out, and the general character of such books with such other statistics . . . as they may deem of general interest and the State Library Board may require." Boards of trustees of Idaho library districts, under Idaho Code 33-2636, also file similar annual reports, which "shall be of such form and contain such information as the state library board may require." The State Library Board, according to Idaho Code 33-2637, "shall, in each of the odd-numbered years and from time to time as requested by the Governor, report to the Governor and the Legislature on the library districts, showing materials added to and withdrawn from the collections and use made of library resources and the cost per capita for library services in each of the library districts."

Oddly enough, Idaho law does *not* specify in similar detail the type of biennial report which the State Library Board must make to the governor. Idaho Code 33-2502 simply says that the State Library Board "shall report biennially to the Governor, with such recommendations as it may deem proper." There is, then, no *requirement* that the State Library Board receive and compile as detailed statistics for ordinary public libraries as it does for library districts.

Currently, Idaho public library and library district statistics, as published annually in the *Idaho Librarian,* give a wide variety of statistical information about the public library setup of Idaho. For most of the libraries and library districts, we are told about the population served, the annual expenditures, per capita expenditures, total book stock, books per capita, circulation per capita, hours open, and number of bookmobile stops. It would probably be safe to hazard that every single public library or library district listed maintains a great many other statistical records. The question is, why? Does knowing how many people come into a library each day result in any change in a library's budget or addition to the staff or other major alterations in that library's makeup? Are figures on binding and mending contributing anything for internal planning purposes? If not, why are these and similar statistics kept?

Obviously, it is unfair to criticize without having definite facts upon which to base such criticism. It may very well be that public libraries and school libraries and college libraries of Idaho keep up only those statistical records which are really necessary. This is something which is not very likely, however.

Look at your own library and see if it is keeping a record of information which is *not* needed, or not making a record of information which *is* needed. In either case, some earnest soul-searching—and action—seems to be in line.

## THE ACCURACY OF FEDERAL ACADEMIC LIBRARY STATISTICS

American academic librarians were overjoyed to receive the annual (1962-63) compilation of academic statistics so early (February) and yet including so high a percentage (70 percent) of the institutions surveyed.[1] A closer examination of the figures revealed, however, certain imperfections and misleading inclusions and omissions that deserve some attention and analysis. This is not a criticism of the Library Services Division but, rather, of a great many of the respondents.

The figures given for "volumes" and for "volumes added," especially in relation to expenditures indicated for "books and other library materials," should cause particular concern. There are, to say the least, many odd figures here. For example, one library, without any footnote of explanation, suddenly increased from less than 25,000 volumes added during 1961-62 to more than three times that number, while the amount shown for "books and other library materials" only increased approximately 50 percent. Upon inquiry, the librarian of this institution stated that "from storage in one attic we removed forty thousand items, some of which have been cataloged, but in the main we are as yet unsure of the number which will be added. The addition of a large number of volumes also included about one-fourth public documents, state and federal, and almost fifty thousand volumes in microtext." The preceding year, neither of these items had been counted; but somehow, in this and other academic libraries, 1962-63 became a great year for including microtexts in "volumes added during the year" and "number of volumes at end of the year."

As a matter of fact, although this particular institution did not bother to state publicly that microtexts were included for the first time, five institutions did so state. Interestingly enough, at the same time, thirteen academic institutions included a footnote stating that their figure for 1962-63 "*excludes* microprints, microcards, microfilms, and other forms of microtext." Just what valid comparisons may be drawn from such utterly different figures is puzzling.

The farther one goes into this labyrinth or wonderland of academic statistics, the "curiouser and curiouser" they get. Under "number of volumes at end of year," only three institutions indicated "estimated" in a footnote. Yet eighty-nine others had figures for this item ending in round numbers. It would take considerable statistical coincidence for so many libraries to come to the end of one particular year with exactly 50,000 or 10,000 or similarly obviously rounded-off figures. Yet they did not admit that their count was estimated; therefore, such figures go in to be compared with the data given by those who have kept very strict count. Upon examination of these eighty-nine institutional reports, one finds that in 1961-62, forty-eight gave rounded-off figures.

The above phenomena merely give grounds for speculation; but one could draw rather definite conclusions from institutions which, when asked specifically, as the questionnaire did, for "number of volumes added during fiscal year (report actual number of volumes acquired, DO NOT subtract volumes withdrawn)" went ahead and gave net figures. How would it have been possible for such institutions to have determined net figures without first having the gross figures? Since they had the gross figures, why did they not give them as requested in the questionnaire?

Further examination is also revealing. Included in the footnotes were various explanations referring to the specific data on "number of volumes at end of year" and "number of volumes added during year." One footnote stated, "excludes microprints," as cited above. Some stated, "an estimated figure"; some stated, "excludes bound periodicals," although the definition of volumes given on page one of the questionnaire stated clearly that "a volume is any printed, typewritten, mimeographed, or processed work, bound or unbound, that has been cataloged or fully prepared for use. Includes microcards, microfilms, microprints, and other forms of microtext." Some stated, "excludes government documents." Some stated, "change in fiscal year on a calendar basis; the number of volumes added is for eighteen-month period." Some stated, "includes only fully cataloged and processed books and periodicals," which sounds like another way of saying "excludes microtexts," but could mean any one of a number of things. One said, "includes data for high school library." Is this a useful statistic for comparative purposes within academic circles? One said, "excludes microfilms and recordings; includes 150,000 microcards." This same institution indicated a little over 150,000 volumes in 1961-62 and over 400,000 for 1962-63. One footnote, which was used by several institutions, stated, "excludes government documents." The instructions on page one of the questionnaire are not clear. The key phrase here is "fully prepared for use." Is a government document that has been assigned any kind of a classification number arranged in any particular way so that it can readily be found and circulated "fully prepared for use"? Different libraries, obviously, differ on this. One library states in a footnote that its listing of "number of volumes at end of year" includes "government serials."

This all seems to indicate the necessity for clarification by definition of what is wanted by the United States Office of Education and by the library profession; a better understanding of what is being asked for is needed by those who fill in the questionnaires. Furthermore, the Office of Education should probably print only those statistics that make sense.

For example, does it make sense to print a particular figure for one year in a category such as "number of volumes at end of year" and a figure next to it for "number of volumes added during year" that could not be compatible? Here are a few examples of such incompatibility.

One institution, in 1961-62, had fewer than 50,000 volumes. It indicates 5,000 volumes added during year and then shows 100,000 volumes at the end of 1962-63. Another showed 60,000 volumes at the end of 1961-62, an addition of 9,000 volumes during 1962-63, and then claims over 130,000 for "number of volumes at end of year" 1962-63. Still another shows less than 90,000, additions of less than 7,000, and a new total of almost 130,000 volumes. This is remarkable arithmetic.

Another school's holdings went from a little over 70,000 to over 100,000 in one year, with "number of volumes added during year" being indicated as under 5,000. How can one add under 5,000 to just over 70,000 and come up with a total of over 100,000? Such figures as these should not be included in a compilation of comparative data. At least, such figures should have been indicated as "estimated." One of the most interesting examples of arithmetic found was of a school that had under 25,000 books in 1961-62, claimed gains of well under 1,000, and then showed the number of volumes at the end of the year at over 35,000!

Correspondence with college librarians leads to the conclusion that the pressure to "keep up with the Joneses" has become, in many instances, so considerable that academic librarians have simply put down figures that look nice rather than accurate figures.[2]

It is to be hoped that the studies now in process under the auspices of the Council on Library Resources, aimed at standardizing library statistics, will be successful. At least, academic librarians should be aware of what they are doing, and the Office of Education should be aware of what it is doing. Putting together indiscriminate statistics into what look like highly organized charts and tables will still produce results and figures which are misleading and inaccurate. What good is the so-called analytic report if the statistics it analyzes are disparate and dissimilar?

William H. Carlson, director of libraries of the Oregon State University, recently said that

figures appearing in such statements [referring to such statements as the ones issued by the Office of Education and the Association of

Research Libraries] are very rough and sometimes, in a comparative sense, even misleading evidence of comparative strength. Sometimes, too, the figures used become suspect. Over decades and centuries the process of adding annual accretions to the accumulated base, and withdrawing the worn out, the lost, and the obsolescent may get badly out of gear. . . . Common-sense observation also indicates that sometimes, either knowingly or unknowingly, figures used have become padded.[3]

Federal academic library statistics as now presented are undoubtedly accurate reports of replies to questionnaires, but a great many of the individual items presented are inconsistent or obviously fallacious. No matter how precise and clear the *questions* asked may be, academic librarians must still rely on the accuracy of *replies.* And no one can examine the 1962-63 figures, especially in relation to previous data, without strong misgivings as to their usefulness for comparative purposes because of the many distortions and inaccuracies they contain.

Action on a nationwide scale toward achieving the obviously impossible—complete and accurate figures on the holdings of *all* academic libraries—is imperative. Each college or university head librarian perhaps has the professional obligation to make a physical inventory of his library's holdings at least once each five years; he certainly should provide accurate annual statistics to the Office of Education.

## ACADEMIC LIBRARY STATISTICS REVISITED

In November, 1964, *College and Research Libraries* published an article concerning academic library statistics which was intended as a one-time study of "certain imperfections and misleading inclusions and omissions that deserve some attention and analysis."[4] The recent publication of *Library Statistics of Colleges and Universities, 1965-66: Institutional Data* compels a return to what were, in 1964, believed to be strictures which would not need repeating as soon as three years later—particularly in light of the aegis under which this newest study was issued, as "Compiled by the Library Administration Division of the American Library Association."

It appears, however, that whether the federal government or the American Library Association prepares college and university statistics, the pitfalls of these publications are so great and likely errors so frequent that the profession might be better off without any so-called national cumulation of figures at all. No lengthy research is necessary to support this point.

The earlier article particularly emphasized the "rather odd figures" given for "volumes" and for "volumes added," especially in relation to expenditures indicated for "books and other library materials." If 1962-63 was considered "rather odd" in this respect, then 1965-66 was, to say the least, weird.

*Item:* A library with 59,000 volumes at the end of 1963-64 reports holding well over 100,000 volumes as of July 1, 1966, despite adding only a few more than 2,500 volumes during 1965-66. This would, of course, mean that during 1964-65, this same library had to have added about 40,000 volumes.

*Item:* Another academic library, with somewhat more than 90,000 volumes as of 1963-64, records nearly 184,000 as of 1965-66.

*Item:* A third, with slightly more than 350,000 volumes in 1963-64 and "volumes added" that year of a little more than 19,000, suddenly becomes "big time," with nearly 550,000 volumes in 1965-66, despite the fact that they indicate fewer then 34,000 volumes added in the same year. One must assume that this institution had around 515,000 in 1964-65, having added the prodigious figure of 160,000 (almost 50 percent) during the year.

Or do these and many similar comparative figures reflect not errors in reporting, but rather (what could be interesting) the fact that since 1963-64 there have been substantial changes in the definition of a volume? An examination of definitions, however, indicates that there has been no such change. For 1963-64, a volume is defined as "A physical unit of any printed, typewritten, handwritten, mimeographed or processed work contained in one binding or portfolio, hardbound or paperbound, which has been classified, cataloged, or otherwise prepared for use. The term includes bound periodical volumes and all non-periodical government documents. All forms of microtext are excluded."[5]

In the 1967 report is found the following definition: "Volume. A physical unit of any printed, typewritten, handwritten, mimeographed or processed work contained in one binding or portfolio, or otherwise prepared for use. The term includes bound periodicals [*sic*] volumes and all non-periodical government documents. All forms of microtext are excluded."[6] This does not *look* like a very substantial change. Actually, the only difference between the two definitions is the omission of the words "hardbound or paperbound, which has been classified, cataloged." Thus there seems to be no evidence of justification for "errors" resulting from a change in the definition of the disputed term *volume*.

Can such variations in reporting be explained in another way? In a preface to the 1967 volume, Theodore Samore says: "the substantial number of incompleted forms necessitated the application of valid editing procedures to retrieve data which would have otherwise been unavailable. Hence, the considerable increase in the number of footnotes, especially those marked 'estimate.'"[7] Since the matter of "estimated" figures is supposedly taken care of by Samore's explanation, let us look over the actual use of estimated figures.

As was pointed out in the 1964 article, the use of rounded-off figures is a fairly clear indication of the use of estimation rather than actual physical or bibliographical count to determine results. The 1965-66 records show use of "estimated" as a footnote (on the matter of volume count) twenty-three times; yet thirty-five other academic institutions show "000" at the end of their volume figures without stating that their figures are estimated.

The figures for "number of volumes added during year" present a similar picture. Of the 1,891 institutions which gave "volumes added" figures, only six footnoted their figures as "estimated"; yet fifty-eight other college and university libraries used rounded-off figures.

Despite the explicit instructions in the questionnaire which was the basis of this report, no fewer than nine *did* include some type of microtext as part of the figures reported under "number of volumes at end of year," of whom three included microtexts added under "number of volumes added during year." Although of all government document holdings only nonperiodical government documents were to be counted as volumes in this survey, one university library "excludes unbound government documents," one college library "excludes U.S. and UN documents," and one university library "excludes nonperiodical government documents." Surely these figures should have been omitted, rather than being counted with an explanatory footnote added, if the totals based on them are supposed to be reliable guides to current trends or situations in academic library resources.

The data concerning microtext holdings in this report are also interesting. The questionnaire gave this definition of microform: "Microform. This includes the form of any library material which has been photographically reduced in size for storage and reproduction purposes, and which must be read with the help of enlarging instruments. The term is synonymous with microtext and includes microfilm, microcard, and microfiche."[8] Column 10 of Table 1 of the 1965-66 report calls for "number of physical units of microform at end of year." Of the respondents, forty-one gave "estimated" figures; three gave "bibliographical count only" (although *physical* units were specifically asked for); one gave "volume count only"; one gave "microfilm only" (which probably means that their microform holdings of documents and manuscripts were not reported, but one cannot be sure). And finally, on this matter, one indicated that it had so many physical units of microform, and so many volumes, but footnoted "data for microform included . . . volumes." It might be asked why this library did not simply subtract one figure from the other and report that total as was asked for, or why the editor did not do it for them.

One must admire the candor of one small church-supported college which reported, "All figures are estimates." Included were such data as the total number of students, the size of the library, the total budget, the number of staff, and even the beginning salary of a library school graduate (fifth year degree without experience). Somehow, however, the mind boggles at *any* academic librarian "estimating" how many students are registered in his institution or how many individuals are on the library staff.

The earlier study of statistics referred to the "wonderland of academic statistics" and said that "the further one goes . . ., the 'curiouser and curiouser' they get."[9] What has been printed in the 1967 report leads one to repeat the comment. When one correlates replies printed under "number of volumes added during year" with the amounts reported as expenditures for "books and other library materials," one runs upon an additional number of unusual figures.

Taking up Table 2, "Operating Expenditures, Personnel, and Beginning Salary . . .," one finds some intriguing footnotes. Under "Wages," for example, twenty-eight give estimated figures, four state that their reports exclude "funds from Federal Work-Study Programs," six say "student assistants only," and one indicates his figures "include all employees paid on an hourly basis." How this latter differs from other reports on "Wages"—since the questionnaire said, "Amounts (including monetary estimates for contributed services) paid to students and to others paid on an hourly basis are listed under 'wages'"—is difficult to understand.

One of the more unusual presentations in Table 2 comes up where total operating expenditures in dollars are asked for. One institution lists a particular specific amount under "total" and then footnotes it as "estimated." Yet none of the other figures for this institution—salaries, cost of library material, binding, or "other"—is marked "estimated." The total of the four figures given is about 3 percent above the total given as "estimated."

Surely the above examples of irresponsible and confused reporting bear out the charges at the beginning of this article. If further evidence is required, one need only look at Table B in the 1965-66 report.[10] The figures for the total number of volumes at the end of the year for the academic library reporting say, most ingenuously, "includes microtext." Yet the questionnaires on which this table is based *exclude* all forms of microtext in asking for "number of volumes at end of year," "number of volumes added during year," and "number of volumes withdrawn during year."

The same Table B is footnoted to indicate that *all* figures for 1966 (that is to say, 1965-66) are "estimated." The previous comments in this article on the values of estimation should be noted again, especially when one realizes that official statements on the state of American academic libraries now are usually based on this *olla podrida* of invalid and unreliable statistics. The figures given for "number of periodicals received" are footnoted as follows: "For 1965-66, the figures are for *Serials* which includes periodicals, annuals, proceedings, transactions, etc." Then why even give 1965-66 figures, since they are based on such hollow shells of fact as are indicated throughout this article, obviously incapable of any meaningful comparison with past data?

In sum, the statistics picture for academic libraries in the United States is at least cloudy, if not psychedelic. Perhaps the task should be returned to the Association of College and Research Libraries, which seemed to do a pretty fair job for a great many years before the computers, the federal government, and the Library Administration Division took over.

In at least one man's judgment, bad—even misleading—statistics are worse than no statistics at all.

## "HALLELUJAH, GIVE US A HAND-OUT AND REVIVE US AGAIN!"

During the last few years the librarians in almost every type of library—school, academic, and public—have become accustomed to the growing amount of federal aid available for various library purposes. Indeed, federal aid to libraries is now at the stage where an entire book was published just to state what federal aid is to be available to elementary and secondary schools and school libraries during fiscal 1967.[11] As this book states, "by using funds that are just one section of the Elementary and Secondary Education Act of 1965, for example, you might develop a remedial reading program, run a pre-school program, develop a guidance program for school dropouts, provide clothing, shoes, or books for needy students, or improve your school library." There are literally hundreds of millions of dollars available right now for libraries, and in various ways Idaho, of course, is affected. Under Title II of the Elementary and Secondary Education Act of 1965, for example, the title which provides funds for library resources, textbooks, and other printed and published instructional material, Idaho is entitled to $370,581. A good share of the materials obtained with this money will obviously go to Idaho school libraries, both public and private.

Under Title III of the National Defense Education Act of 1958 (revised), which includes funds for "instructional equipment and materials in such fields as science, mathematics, history, civics, geography, modern foreign languages, English, reading, and economics," Idaho, for fiscal 1966, is entitled to $400,000.

Idaho public libraries which happen to be located in cities which have institutions of higher education may hire students working under the College Work-Study Program by paying only one-tenth of their salaries, 90 percent being paid by the federal government. Hundreds of thousands of dollars are available for this purpose throughout the state.

Obviously, this amount of money coming into Idaho has had, is having, and will have appreciable effects on the operations of our libraries of every type. The above is only a partial listing of the funds available to libraries of all sorts in Idaho, but should be enough to indicate the breadth and depth of aid available.

Unfortunately, this largess is not an unmixed blessing. Too many of the libraries of Idaho are going to deteriorate into the level suggested by the title of this article, based on the famous "Hallelujah, I'm a Bum!" parody. All of the federal money is intended as a stimulus and a corrective, with the hopeful idea that local funds and state funds will ultimately be the means for achieving the same good ends that are being fostered by the federal funds.

Idaho librarians certainly cannot say that they are doing all they should be doing in the way of getting local and state funds, so long as full advantage is not taken of the possibilities for local and state funds. As a specific example, look at the implementation that has been made of an action by the 1963 State Legislature amending Section 33-2601 of the Idaho Code so that public libraries may now tax up to five mills rather than the previously established three mills. This law was approved on March 14, 1963, but how many libraries have taken advantage of it?

According to the latest figures available from the State Library, of the ninety-nine public libraries of record in the state of Idaho, only eleven are now collecting a tax of over three mills, and only three are collecting the full five mills permissible under the law. Of course, even with the full five mills, many small communities in Idaho do not provide enough assessed evaluation, and minimal ALA standards for public libraries can certainly not be met. There is still a need for more cooperation between public libraries in particular areas of the state; and also there is definitely need for recognition by public libraries in Idaho of the need for as much use as possible being made of the services and holdings of the State Library.

Of the fifteen library districts now in existence in Idaho, only a very few are taxing up to their legal limit of five mills. Incidentally, the story of library districts in Idaho may well serve as a salutary reminder of the basic needs which are as yet unmet in our state. In 1955, when the original library district bill was passed, something over 50 percent of Idaho's population had no library service; now, 11 years later, there are still 227,265 Idaho residents—34 percent of our population—without any library service. At this rate of approximately 1 percent improvement per year, it would take another 34 years—up to the year 2000—before all of our citizens had any public library service whatsoever. This is another example of where local initiative has been lacking.

On the academic institution level, of the eight Idaho college and university libraries reporting, only half are, as of latest figures available, getting the 5 percent of their institutional funds that college libraries should have as a very minimum, by ALA standards, to provide the services and reading materials that academic students and faculty should have. And this 5 percent figure is recommended only where there are already collections of a suitable size and quality available; otherwise, much more of the institutional budget should go to library budgets.

Our school libraries are in the worst shape of any of the various types of libraries within our state, in terms of provisions made on the local level for library budgeting. The American Library Association standards for school library programs, as issued in 1960, asked for an annual budget for printed materials from school libraries of $1,000 to $1,500 in books in schools having 200 to 249 students and from $4 to $6 per student in schools having 250 or more students. Please bear in mind even this would mean only about one book per student could be added to the school library each year. In addition, the standards call for supplementary funds for encyclopedias, unabridged dictionaries, magazines, newspapers, and pamphlets. Original collections of books in the school library are supposed to be in the range of at least 3,000 books for schools having 200 to 499 students, at least 5,000 books for schools having 500 to 1,499 students, and at least 3 books per student for schools having 1,500 or more students.

There are NO school libraries in the state of Idaho which match the minimum standards set by the American Library Association in 1960. Even with federal funds which have come in from the National Defense Education Act of 1958 and from the Elementary and Secondary Education Act of 1965, it is still true that most school libraries in the state are far below minimum levels. Unfortunately, there are too many local school districts still not aware of the importance of the school libraries, which are given far below minimum budgets. Even where the book supply is fairly adequate, no provision is made for keeping up a good periodical collection, a minimum newspaper collection, a minimum pamphlet collection, and various materials such as films and filmstrips, tape recordings, pictures and slides, and other audiovisual materials.

Putting it very bluntly, the residents of Idaho are getting what they are willing to pay for on a local and statewide level, so far as library service is concerned. Those residents who are complaining about "federal control" and various other epithets aimed at federal aid have only themselves to thank for the coming of federal funds into our state. The trustees in the library district or the city public library area who have gone along year after year with the very, very minimum in tax levies for public libraries are the ones who should be asking, "Why haven't we gone up to five mills? What is the relative importance of libraries in our city or library district?" The school boards in local districts who have gladly accepted federal aid but have at the same time complained about it are complaining about conditions that they themselves have brought into being, which required, in the national interest, the passing of various federal laws which made funds available from federal taxes to support the libraries which could well have been supported by local effort. The colleges, whether public or private, which are now yearly looking forward to the federal "handouts" of grants of money for building purposes and for reading materials, are the same colleges whose administrations and boards have not made sure that the colleges are even, on a very minimal basis, well enough staffed and equipped to provide the services and reading materials that Idaho college students should have.

Federal funds for school libraries and public libraries and academic libraries in Idaho should only come to us until we do meet the minimum standards and until support on the state and local level is at least adequate to permit the minimal functioning of Idaho libraries of all types. It may be that all Idaho libraries of all types will never meet the minimum standards (which themselves will regularly move upward). There is some talk on a national level of perpetuating federal library aid to public libraries, at least, on a 15 percent basis; that is, 60 percent support from local sources, 25 percent from state sources, and 15 percent from federal funds. In my opinion this is not a realistic goal. I would hope that federal funding of all types of libraries would be considered only as a temporary supplement and should not be expected to continue indefinitely. Local and state sources SHOULD provide more support for all publicly supported Idaho libraries, although certainly all federal aid available should be used.

## NOTES

1. This figure increased to 90 percent in June, with the ALA-LAD published supplement. All figures in this section are based on the original documents.

2. The state university library supervised by this writer has well over 300,000 government documents. These are *not* included in the totals reported to the federal government because such publications, although they are kept in bureau order and within each bureau by type of publication and then numerically, are not considered by us as being "fully ready for use" in terms of the government definition. Those few documents in the writer's library which will get better use if they are fully cataloged, specified, and placed among the books in the regular collection *are* included in the totals, but no others. Also, in this library, no microtexts in any form have been included in final reported totals, mainly because of the confusion concerning how they are to be counted.

3. William H. Carlson, "The Field Headquarters of the Mind: Measures of Library Excellence," *Improving College and University Teaching* (Spring, 1964), pp. 68-69.

4. Eli M. Oboler, "The Accurary of Federal Academic Library Statistics," *College and Research Libraries* (November, 1964), pp. 494-97.

5. U.S., Office of Education, *Library Statistics of Colleges and Universities, 1963-64, Institutional Data,* circular no. 769, OE-15023-64 (Washington, D.C.: Government Printing Office, 1965), p. 4.

6. American Library Association, Library Administration Division, comp., *Library Statistics of Colleges and Universities, 1965-66, Institutional Data* (Chicago: American Library Association, 1967), p. 3.

7. Ibid., p. 2.

8. Ibid., p. 3.

9. Oboler, "The Accuracy of Federal Academic Library Statistics," p. 494.

10. "Summary of College and University Library Statistics for Academic Years 1959-65," pp. 6-9.

11. Ruth Ann Roney, *The Doubleday Guide to Federal Programs: 1966-67—Elementary and Secondary Schools and School Libraries* (Garden City, N.Y.: Doubleday, 1966).

# 6 RESOLUTION

## SOME THOUGHTS ON ACADEMIC LIBRARIANSHIP

### The Omniscient Librarian

There is an old wheeze which claims that all mankind is divided into two categories: those who divide mankind into two categories and those who don't. I am afraid that I am of category one: my tendency is to divide, if not *all* mankind, then at least all librarians into two categories—those who are academic librarians and those who are not. I am well aware of the "core" theory of library education, which has as its basis that there is only a single, basic "core" to library science and all else is peripheral. But I beg to differ.

It is really not very difficult to define "academic" -ness. It is clearly not any one of the rather negative, common dictionary definitions. Certainly no librarian in a college or university wants to be considered "theoretical: speculative," as one popular lexicographer's monument has it. How about "scholarly to the point of being unaware of the outside world"? The Saint-Beuvean ivory tower concept obviously comes to the fore here. Still worse: "formalistic; conventional." No insight there.

So, perforce, we are left with definition number one: "of, pertaining to, or characteristic of a school." The *academic* quality of the academic librarian is related to his or her connection with his or her academy, his college, his university. The relation, to be truly appropriate, one would conjecture, must be not to behave—whether in an administrative or ancillary position—in such a manner as to be contrary to the goals and spirit of the institution where one works. There is no place in academic librarianship for the prima donna, the maverick type.

Let me hasten to say that this is not to contradict the self-description given in the subtitle of this volume. One need not go off the rails completely; or, to carry on the same metaphor, one can certainly keep on the track, while changing speeds, of eventual goals.

To illustrate with a concrete example, I see no benefit from the head librarian of an academic library who rushes into computerization when the rest of his college or university is not far beyond the quill pen. Leadership is one thing; anarchism is another.

My three decades or so of academic library experience has been, I must hasten to admit, somewhat limited. I have been an academic librarian, and *only* an academic librarian, all my professional life. As such, I look with jaundiced eye indeed on the vita and, if I may say so, *lack* of vita of all of my profession who have not labored in the groves of Academe. Now there, doesn't that sound stuffy enough and "ivory tower" enough to prove my bona fides in my branch of the profession?

"Groves of Academe," indeed! More like the stables of Augeas, that unhappy king of mythological Greece whose vast and reeking stables, housing 3,000 oxen, and which had not been cleaned for thirty years, Hercules was forced to clean as one of his dozen labors. And if you think my metaphor is over-rhetorical or farfetched, let me ask you, fellow academic librarians, how easy have *your* contacts been with faculty and students and administration through *your* working career? Perhaps the Herculean tasks we academicians must, each in his own way, perform are not as readily performed by such facile expedients as Hercules' own, diverting a river through them. Or perhaps, to carry the figure just a little further, the river of expertise has been steadily flowing through your private Augean Stables all the time, and no desperate, sudden remedy is necessary. If so, offer, if not à la Socrates, a cock to Aescalapius, then perhaps an appropriate oblation to Mnemosyne, who should be (if she isn't) the object of every librarian's worship.[1]

But back to the point of the singularity, the uniqueness of academic librarians among all the various areas of the profession. There are, of course, many respects wherein the librarian in a college or university library differs not at all from the school or the public or the special librarian. It should not be necessary to recapitulate these herein.

But there are some responsibilities and some specific tasks incident to fulfilling these responsibilities which I believe are unique to the academic librarian. To begin with, the academic librarian must be at least intellectually well enough equipped to have a general background in the whole world of knowledge. Where the public librarian deals with the general public, almost from the cradle to the grave, the academic librarian must deal with students and researchers, a rather different clientele. He should have the broadest possible liberal arts background so that he can at least understand and be able to communicate with, in a general way, that clientele. He certainly must know the history of higher education, as well as its place in the entire educational system of this country and, indeed, of the world. He should, and I am speaking here particularly of the top administrator or administrators in an academic library, understand the workings of the source from which the library budget flows—and this gets into finance, economics, and political science. On today's campus, no longer elitist but having its share of ethnic minority group faculty and students, he needs to be something of a sociologist and psychologist. In fact, today's academic librarian really needs to be on the order of the major general in Gilbert and Sullivan's *Pirates of Penzance,* who claimed to have "information vegetable, animal, and mineral." He must be both a bookman and, to coin a phrase, a *people* man. To be a properly educated and educable academic librarian is beyond human capacity, but the individual who assumes that role at least can try.

One of the most difficult assignments for any academic librarian is to deal fairly and reasonably with the always present problem of too little book money and too many faculty members trying to get what they believe to be their fair, reasonable share of that inadequate amount. I can't imagine a more thorough, more logical set of arguments than J. Periam Danton gives in favor of permitting the professional library staff of an academic library to do most of the book selection for its institution.[2] Published more than a decade ago, Danton's book has yet to permeate where it really counts, to the minds of department chairmen and library committee members; but I am thrilled to report at least one dean of my acquaintance actually admitted the validity of the Danton arguments, when I narrated them to him.

And why not? They're cogent, informed, and—if they would only be read and appreciated in the correct academic circles—potentially very effective. What are they? I really hesitate (if you haven't read the Danton book, you should) to try to miniaturize or condense *his* comments, but here goes. The most important section of the book, in my mind, is the one in which he criticizes the so-called departmental allocations by formula, for a number of reasons.[3]

First, he claims, and rightly so, "that no satisfactory formula for the division of funds has ever been devised." (If any reader of this book knows of one, where has he been hiding this pearl without price of unknown wisdom?) Then he deplores the removal of the basic responsibility for book selection from the library, "where it administratively, philosophically, and usually logically belongs," and turning that burden over to the teaching faculty, "who cannot be held responsible or accountable." I've often wondered how faculty members would react if we librarians were to decide their curricula or their grading systems for them. Danton minces no words in stating that he doubts that the faculty as a group can really "be relied upon to perform the task of selection regularly, systematically, thoroughly, and objectively." We *can*; or if we can't, what are we doing in academic librarianship?

Danton continues by pointing out what is almost a truism—that if we rely on the faculty's selection, we are bound to have "unbalanced, uncoordinated selection" and that books will be bound to be purchased on "a personal interest basis." Next he stresses the loss in flexibility, which denies the ability to purchase large collections or to meet sudden new demands or the capacity to build up in known areas of weakness. He reminds us that using the allocation technique is almost sure to cause "some neglect of overlapping, interstitial, and peripheral area works." Books on the oceans, for example—aside from libraries in coastal cities, perhaps! Then he deplores the so frequently encountered practice, normal under the allocation system, of what he calls "inconsidered ordering"—orders made in haste and without much selectivity, merely to use up unexpended funds, near the end of a fiscal year. Finally, he questions whether departmental allocations are ever large enough to permit buying "highly important but very expensive multi-volume works."

The most common objections to leaving book funds in the control of the librarian or the library staff are that the librarians do not have the expertise of the teaching faculty and that any system not involving fixed allocations will necessarily result in one or a few departments "hogging" all the available funds for their particular interests.

The first objection is certainly becoming passé with the advent of the double-master's requirement in many academic libraries; the second implies utter stupidity on the part of the library administration.

But the question still remains in the vast majority of academic libraries; who buys the books? And it will take a long, long time before the optimum solution—a mixture of better communication of the cogent facts and arguments from the library to the faculty and administration, of better professional and subject preparation of the library staff, and of mutual trust—will be even close to being a universal reality. Just so long as librarians abdicate their responsibility as collection builders, they are not living up to one of their basic professional obligations; and the academic library collections in America will be the worse for that widespread abdication of that responsibility.

## The Computer Versus the Real Thing

One of the bounden duties of today's academic librarian is to understand and use the computer. For one trained when the use of the ball-point pen was still a glimmer in the future, the insouciance of the current library school graduate, glib in such esoterica as Fortran and permuted title indexes and the various and distinct benefits of line-printers and phototypesetters and cathode-ray tubes, condescendingly expert in his or her references to a myriad of acronyms and other mnemonic devices referring to goshknowswhat— for such a one the Computer demands a capital *C*. But not necessarily capital funds from the increasingly hard-won library budget.

There are too many well-documented horror tales still floating around, of the pitfalls of the unchecked, not well planned, undue computerization of academic library activities. Cataloging and acquisitions? Well, maybe. Circulation? Probably. But reference, "information searching" (as current lingo has it), not just yet. *If* it's practical, it costs too much. If it's usable, it still can't match the lightning brain and memory of that precious jewel among librarians, the well-trained, experienced reference librarian. Yes, I know. I'm Polonius *revividus,* neither the first to try a new gadget nor the last to put the tried and true one aside. But I'm not floundering in a sea of computer-based professional embarrassment either!

The mentor of OCLC, Frederick G. Kilgour, has informed us (via a 1967 book to which he contributed), that even in those early days of the computer-library liaison, "most librarians do not yet understand computation and computer people are equally ignorant of librarianship."[4] Despite a hundred library school courses and a thousand workshops and myriad items in library literature, this is still basically true. I still cannot see a *real* librarian (whatever that is) buying the completely computer-based information organization and handling theory. The machine, I prejudicedly recognize, can do the busy work; but can it do the brain work? I doubt it. As is probably evident, on this matter (as on others) I'm probably conditioned by my generational milieu; but I just *may* be right.

## Reading for Culture and Fun

Another obligation of the academic library is to satisfy the extracurricular needs of its patrons, so far as is reasonable and possible. Merely putting out a new batch of books on occasion hardly satisfies this requirement. Nor, really, does a separate browsing room or area or set of shelves really do it, although this might help.

With the best will in the world, no group of individualistically inclined, highly specialized faculty can, as individuals or en masse, produce a balanced, culturally satisfying book and periodical collection. There are all too many faculty who are so tunnel-visioned that they will not even order books in their own general subject area but insist on getting publications which are really extremely highly specialized. Given enough faculty and money and time, this might very well produce, by sheer weight of numbers, a fairly balanced, wide-ranging collection which would include the enjoyable and enlightening books of the day or month or year. But it is really up to the professional library staff to perform the important task of supplying and making readily available not just the best sellers but the notable and significant and, on occasion, some of the trivial but readable current books.

Some academic librarians, I am well aware, flinch at the very thought of buying, for example, an *I'm O.K.; You're O.K.* kind of "pop" psychology book or supplying books on such hardly esoteric topics as backpacking or chess playing. "We can't fill the needs of the faculty," they say; but what about the needs of the student? He or she isn't studying every minute, we know; and if the broad, background, cultural needs of a well-rounded culture must be supplied, then recreation should be included. There is an absolutely undocumentable statistic I heard once, to the effect that those who go to college for four years (and stop there) read no more than a single book a year, on the average, throughout the rest of their lives. If that is true, then it is certainly important that within the four years during which they are doing a good deal of reading, a wide choice be afforded for reading by the academic library. The Great Books should be there, and so should the great detective stories and even a few books of *Pogo* and *Peanuts*. Let the library be more—much more—than a dour, dank place for (I loathe the term) "supplementary reading." The influx of independent study courses, the gradual aging of academia's clientele as our population gets older on the average and wants and needs more college training, the sheer availability of inexpensive paperbacks—these and many other reasons point toward letting the academic library be a cornucopia of reading riches, not a vault of reserved books.

### The Knowledge Explosion

There are about 50 million scientific papers now available. This "stockpile" is increasing at the annual rate of about 9 percent per year and has done so since the end of World War II. About 70 percent of this mountain of material comes from non-U.S. sources.[5] Just what is the obligation of the academic library to, for example, the research chemist on his campus—undergraduate or graduate student or faculty member? Is all of this material listed in *Chemical Abstracts* and so known to the chemical researcher *suitable,* required to be *on hand,* to be asked for in original or copied form from another library, no matter how far away that library is or what it costs to get that material?

No matter how you consider it, it is a difficult problem with which to attempt to cope. Interlibrary loans are, at best, an unsatisfactory tool (at the tender mercies of the U.S. Postal Service) beginning to get quite expensive or even to be denied the cooperation of some institutions. Computerized reference service—BALLOTS, *New York Times,* or whatever—is very expensive, so much so that only a comparatively few individual institutions can afford such service. Various ways of dealing with this are being discussed or are actually being tried, but none seems satisfactory. Short of some kind of article birth control, the problem will stay with us. Exactly what *can* we do?

Howard Mumford Jones put the problem of the scholar vis-à-vis the knowledge explosion very concretely: "If one were to believe a good many scholars, the duty of the librarian is to get them whatever they want because they want it. The resulting policy of competition and pressure means, in extreme cases, that the library is distinguished for nothing and merely competent in everything."[6] And I question only one phrase in those statements, "in extreme cases." The very fact that library accreditation requirements the country over use the term "adequate" as a description of desired academic library collections should verify my view. We *do* have mostly "merely competent" and very few indeed "distinguished" academic libraries in America. And part of the blame must rest with faculty pressure for what I call the "coral reef" kind of library.

There are many distinctive tropical isles bordered by coral reefs, and biologists (starting with Charles Darwin) have made studies of their origins. The scientific consensus seems to be expressed as follows: "the young or larvae of the coral polyps, of pin-head size ... [which] may chance to reach a reefless share of firm rock in water of proper temperatures ... may attach themselves there and grow, at first in small patches, later in larger communities."[7] Aside from the reference to self-directing, doesn't this sound exactly like the kind of academic libraries which have grown without real direction or selection? Professor X says, "Get this." Professor Y says, "Buy that." Professor Z says, "Get everything available," on something else. Within the obvious limitations of funds, availability of the item or items requested, and, on occasion, consideration of space, most academic librarians keep adding their little bits of coral and more. And then the library needs an annex or an addition. Then, even more inevitably (if that is possible) a new library building is needed.

### Cui bono? Travel or Interlibrary Loan?

Some years ago a very ingenious solution was proposed for the most prevalent and enduring problem in every academic library, at least so far as the faculty is concerned. No library, no matter how large, no matter how balanced or how varied its collection, can possibly match all or even *nearly* all the incredibly diverse demands of those conducting research in every possible field of knowledge. But a solution which still makes a lot of sense has been proffered in different places at various times which, unfortunately, seems not to get much further than the recommendation stage.

What has been suggested is that faculty members who for purposes of valid and necessary research need to use a relatively large amount or number of materials from a particular library should be given travel funds by their institutions to do so, preferably without the requirement of a sabbatical leave for this purpose. Such details as length of stay, maximum permitted cost, and travel distances to be approved will need clarification. But shouldn't it be possible to send the researcher *to* the library, in some cases, rather than try to fit research into the Procrustean bed of interlibrary loan and its obvious limitations?

Surely this makes a lot of sense. There is just no way that interlibrary loans or even the most elaborate system of on-line computer terminals and data-based communications can possibly substitute for an actual visit to a library which has broad, expansive materials in a particular area which the researcher is seeking. The ability to use a library's own subject catalog, the even more helpful technique of browsing among the books and profiting from the curiously effective benefits of serendipity, and, it should go without saying, the benefit of using the brains of the resident library staff are incontrovertible arguments in favor of using a library oneself. Of course, travel to and from libraries would cost money, but so does everything and anything connected with research.

Speaking of travel, it would be, in Shakespearean phrase, certainly "a consummation devoutly to be wished" if professional—and, on occasion, especially qualified, paraprofessional and clerical—staff members were more easily able to attend library association conferences and useful workshops; most colleges and universities would profit a great deal more from the use of a relatively small amount of money added to the always inadequate library travel fund than from the usually comparatively readily available capital funds for books and other library materials.

A reasonable approach might be to supply sufficient travel funds so that every professional staffer could attend at least one national or regional association conference and the state conference or a workshop each year. Let's use the latest available national figure for professional staffing of academic librarians, 3.7 in each library, and let's assume that at least $500 should be allotted annually for travel for each one. We then would need $1,850, which is really not very much of the total average budget, as per the latest available figures of $304,581 average total budget for each academic library in the United States.[8]

## The Spirit of Service

What motivates the academic librarian ultimately decides what motivates the academic library. What the academic library is like eventually decides the spirit of the academic institution of which it is a part. Cliché-packed anatomical analogies as to the part which the library plays in its parent institution, considered as the central body, accomplish little except perhaps an opportunity for easy reference to the library in presidential speeches. But whether considered as a stereotype, cliché, or any other kind of obviosity, the library must be given its fair place in the campus scheme of things, or the entire institution will suffer.

Show me a library whose head and staff are rarely, if ever, considered or consulted when new, significant educational programs are being planned, and I'll show you a campus where the new programs are either half-baked or botched up. Or, putting it more positively, when the head librarian is given his or her proper administrative place—on a par, at least with the academic deans (if not with the vice-president, the provosts, or whatever the latest management title may be)—then the institution and its leaders are putting the academic library into its proper perspective.

Please do not, after reading this, accuse me of being in the ranks of the admirers of that perennial chimera, the so-called library-college. When I was young and callow, I, too, saw some possibilities in this most unlikely of potentialities. But I have, to date, seen no examples of where this form of organization was worked in even a medium-sized academic institution—say, 8,000 to 20,000 students.

And, idealistic as I believe I still am, I'm just not naïve enough to accept the thesis that most colleges and universities will eventually *truly* center around their libraries. There may be a few now, and there may be a few more in years to come; but the library-college, in my opinion, will never replace the present academic structure in America.

What *is* that structure? What *should* it be? Most of the discussion of the academic library's future in current library literature seems to center around two features, management devices and communication devices. I think neither is as important as what I referred to just above as the "spirit" of academia. The spirit of true education—of the unfettered communication of information and informed opinion —must, in the long run, reign, before the academic library will really have the chance to show what it can do. Convince the faculty, the administrators, the state and private boards of trustees that libraries are more than show-worthy giant edifices, more than convenient gathering places for the gadgets and gizmos of the world of education, more than piles and stacks and shelves of books and periodicals and pamphlets and records and documents and a gallimaufry of audiovisual formats. Convince the campus that the academic library is, first of all, a place for *service* (that old, old, old-fashioned concept), and the academic library will take its rightful place on any campus.

## The Academic Library's Relative Importance

The most important and potentially fruitful study of American higher education, that made by the Carnegie Commission on Higher Education during the early 1970s, well illustrates the academic library's lack of central significance by its almost steady neglect of that topic. This multivolume work includes no single section on libraries, but does have a few nuggets of wisdom and advice concerning libraries scattered here and there in the many reports it contains. Perhaps the most important is negatively slanted. The volume on *The More Effective Use of Resources,* which was the result of a continuing financial crisis of U.S. higher education in the early 1970s, said, in its discussion of how to save money within colleges and universities, "What not to do is as important as what to do. We consider it unwise, however tempting in the short run, to cut such items as: necessary maintenance, library expenditures for new books and for journals, student aid without at least making loans available."[9] It is good to see the injunction about *not* cutting library materials and expenditures, plainly and concretely stated. Now, how many top administrators, presidents, and board members will *heed* this expert advice?

A quite interesting comparable conclusion, this time based on a nationwide survey of faculty members, showed that of nine alternatives for "first cut" in case of the need for campus budget retrenchment, funds for libraries and laboratories were approved by only 4 percent (eighth among the nine), with 58 percent listing this category as among the last to be cut. Only "funds directed primarily to the teaching program" had a higher priority to the nationwide sample of teaching faculty in the Ladd-Lipset Survey.[10] Also, funds for libraries and laboratories were given a higher priority than research expenditures, and as first on the list (73 percent) for "first cut" if fiscal cutbacks were necessary. Again, as in the case of the Carnegie recommendations, one cannot feel too reassured. When push comes to shove, will *your* library budget be cut first or last?

This, I suppose, depends on a great many other factors than survey or commission opinions. You are most likely to be cut if you (a) have money to "spare" from your budget, and/or (b) you have not been providing services which your campus found essential.

The library in a publicly supported institution which insists on such obvious luxuries as highly expensive, funded-from-normal-budget rare book collections or ostentatiously "plush" furniture and office fixings is a very likely target for the cost cutters. If your collection is not reflective of campus and curricular needs, if your services are grudgingly, even coldly, given, if your rapport with students and faculty and administration is that in name only—you *should* expect the worst.

In this connection, some recent federal educational statistics may be of interest. *The Digest of Educational Statistics: 1975 Edition* tells us that the latest available figures for 1972-73 show that library operating expenditures of some $867 million (in total) of the nearly 3,000 libraries reporting meant only 4.1 percent of the total institutional expenditures for educational and general purposes.[11] And this was a drop of exactly 1/10 of 1 percent from the 1968-69 percentage for libraries. With the steady rise in costs of books and nonprint items and personnel and every other item or individual related to libraries, we who are academic librarians have actually managed to go down in our ratio of achievement in competition for the academic dollar. This is really something to brag about, I suppose.

There is an old Roman Catholic prayer which says, *"Peccavi! Peccavi! Peccavi! Mea maxima culpa!"* In other words, "I have sinned! I have sinned! I have sinned! My very great fault!" You might not want to beat your breast and admit crimes you personally have not committed, but *somebody* in our profession has goofed. That 4.1 percent versus 4.2 percent didn't just happen.

We are, to varying degrees, all guilty. We have not used our public relations knowledge and techniques and outlets to the very best possible advantage. We have not "sold" our budget controllers on the sad facts of rising library costs and equally rising demands on libraries. We have not convinced our students or the teaching faculty or the administration of our true importance in the campus scheme of things.

And things are not likely to get better. Another recent federal publication, *Projections of Education Statistics to 1984-85,* shows that capital outlay by American institutions of higher education is not predicted to increase.[12] Six hundred million dollars were spent for this purpose (a good share, of course, for library materials) in 1974-75.

We can do a great many things to help ourselves which we undeniably are not now doing. I get quite unhappy when, on accreditation trips such as I've been privileged to undertake for the Northwest Association of Secondary and Higher Schools since the 1960s, time and time again I find that the institution's president hardly ever acknowledges the existence of the library on his campus as being worth mentioning. Self-reports usually say something like "the library is doing a fine job," and let it go at that. Surely it is the responsibility of the head librarian to see to it that every possible detail of his operations which needs airing is there for the accreditation team to review. I have actually seen *single*-page library self-studies included within *200*-page institutional self-studies. This is either careless neglect or sheer foolhardiness, in my opinion.

*Librarianship and Imagination*

If we agree with Alfred North Whitehead that "education is the acquisition of the art of the utilization of knowledge," then the place of the academic library in the realm of higher education is almost self-evident.[13] The library is the repository of knowledge, as that is available in print and nonprint forms. The faculty, it must follow, is the group in the academic world which teaches the student how to use that knowledge which is available (a) from them, (b) via the laboratory or independent inquiry and investigation, and (c) from the library. Placing the library third in this sequence is not to derogate its importance.

The academic library is the only place on a campus where the assembled facts and opinions of present and past generations are gathered together in one spot (presuming those abominations to organized thought, the small departmental libraries, are not in existence) and organized systematically for effective use. The artificial distinctions of classification do, it is true, sometimes separate books which seem linked; but the proper sort of cataloging (including subject headings and cross-references which are designed to illuminate and relate, not obfuscate and divide, knowledge) will enable the educator and the student to use the library to the best possible advantage.

Whitehead sees the only justification for a university in what it does which "preserves the connection between knowledge and the zest of life, by uniting the young and the old in the imaginative consideration of learning." "Imaginative consideration of learning." Now there's a phrase which should be over the doors, at least figuratively speaking, of every academic library. It is so very easy indeed to lose that zest, that imagination that "atmosphere of excitement, arising from imaginative consideration, [which] transforms knowledge," as Whitehead stresses.[14] It is not an easy task to use imagination, as the philosopher recommends, "by eliciting the general principles which apply to the facts, as they exist, and then by an intellectual survey of alternative possibilities which are consistent with those principles" to cause the student "to construct an intellectual vision of a new world."

Surely those are high and inspiring principles for any academician to follow. Now, let's get down to earth and follow the unfortunately more or less typical John W. Dryasdust, director of libraries of the State University of Dullsville. His library is planned for the sole benefit of the library staff's needs and comfort; books are made as hard to get to as possible, and no signs or handbooks or guiding leaflets are provided to help the weary knowledge seeker.

The Dryasdust kind of library has the books the faculty asked for, and just about only those. Perhaps there are a few more or less obvious basic reference works, but that is it. When there is an opportunity to get books in some micro- or macroform which the average student or instructor will dislike, even resent, Dryasdust is always the first to embrace that opportunity. In the Dryasdust lexicon, "service" is the forgotten word.

Now of course this is an exaggerated, a phantasmic picture. No modern academic library would in any way be like the Dullsville model. But the possibility is always there; the academic librarian who goes a-whoring for the latest in library "trendy" items or methods all too often will forget his basic, essential fidelity to the cause of making knowledge available.

To quote Whitehead once more, "The gift which the University has to offer is the old one of imagination, the lighted torch which passes from hand to hand. It is a dangerous gift, which has started many a conflagration. If we are timid as to that danger, the proper course is to shut down our universities."[15] Without imagination, tempered with reasonableness and practicality, no academic library can either, really, be truly academic or a library. And the academic librarian who must assume the burden of responsibility for the day-by-day operation of the academic library must himself have the service spirit and the imaginative zest and zeal for which Whitehead calls. Otherwise, if we don't shut down the university, at the very least we should shut down the library!

## Conclusions

Mass higher education in America since World War II, featured by a growth of the percentage of American youth eighteen to twenty-one attending some kind of academic institution all the way from around 10 percent in 1945 to over 30 percent in 1975, has had a concomitant effect on American libraries and librarianship. When expenditures of academic libraries are up to nearly $1 billion a year (even in inflated dollars), it has, of course, meant much more attention to the minutiae of budget administration and machine operation than to the true work of the library—exciting the imagination of the library's patrons to the fulfillment of the Whitehead notion of the welding together of imagination and experience.

Naturally, the academic librarian must be basically a bibliophile. He may also be a systems-ophile, a computer lover, and an instructional resources nut—but he really does have to have read, and to continue to read and enjoy—and stimulate others to read—the worthwhile books of the past and the present. How else can he fulfill his responsibilities as one of the (if not *the*) intellectual leaders of his campus? What other field in Academe even attempts to resist the current and seemingly popular fragmentation of knowledge?

We cannot facilely pass on our professional sins and derelictions to the teaching faculty; for example, no worthwhile institution of higher education's library collection can be anything but amorphous, undirected, and unbalanced if the professional library staff does not at least make an effort to participate in basic book selection. So-called get-'em-all policies can only contribute to the deprofessionalization of the librarians and the de-qualitization of what is available to the library. Surely the broad training and experience of academic librarians, with or without that second master's degree or that quite infrequent doctor's degree, is at least as valuable an asset as the highly specialized book knowledge of the teaching professor.

These remarks are not particularly for the academic librarian in one type of academic library or another—university, college, or community college. Indeed, they should be appropriate for the eager neophyte or the exhausted veteran in any or all of the fields of Academe. All academic librarians share basic responsibilities—to their profession, their milieu, and themselves. This is not as clichéful a remark as it might seem.

Because of the known peripateticness of academic library life, there is an unfortunate tendency for librarians who come to particular libraries and particular colleges and universities to see their posts as temporary and therefore important only as stepping stones. Stepping up on stones is not too bad a way to get to the higher levels, literally speaking; but beware lest the stones, metaphorically speaking, be a matter of a number of two or three year stints where the wandering individual hardly cares about his library, let alone the institution of which it is a part.

One hallmark of the truly academic librarian is his or her ability, willingness, even *desire* to cooperate, to work in tandem, not independently, with the faculty, the administration, and, particularly, with the students. If the student body of Stodgy University shows signs of being "with it," it really won't hurt the library or its staff or the faculty to go along with at least some of the youthful ideas which emerge. For example, why must every possible inch of reading space have actual furniture? Students—if it is any news to any observant librarians who may read this—enjoy sitting, reclining, or being in just about any kind of posture on a carpeted floor with or without chairs or other furnishings. Fancy, expensive chairs or carrels are really not essential for student comfort. This is just one librarian's trivial but characteristic example of how an empathetic academic librarian can best indicate concretely that empathy.

It is, after all, the individual student who should be the greatest concern of any truly professional academic librarian. Whitehead has said that "the valuable intellectual development is self-development."[16] Whatever our particular share in the library enterprise, our constant and overwhelming goal must be to help the student (that term subsumes the undergraduate, the graduate, and the faculty member) to develop his own intellect. No amount of jargon-filled talk of electronic wizardry, of modern management technics, of miniaturization or networking can substitute for a spirit of service.

Yes, service—a nearly forbidden word in the lexicon of librarianship, especially academic librarianship. What the new generation of "with it" academic librarians seem to have either never learned or to have quickly forgotten is that there is little if any indication that the modern academic institution will ever become the library-centered place called for by the totally unrealistic library-college movement. The energy being expended on this kind of ultra-idealistic, Utopian dream might well, in my opinion, be better devoted to making the best of the library *in* the college, not the library *as* the college. American higher education could, of course, always benefit by innovation; one very welcome such idea would be to concentrate less on gadgetry and organizational manipulation—including that real chimera, participatory library management—and more on doing some very old-fashioned but important functions, none of which is dependent on the use of computer terminals or audiovisual carrels. I agree with Whitehead that "the best education is to be found in gaining the utmost information from the simplest apparatus."[17] Perhaps greater philosophers will come along some day with more alluring, more seemingly acceptable generalizations on the best way to train our youth for life. But Whitehead will do, for me, for now.

## NOTES

1. Or have you (who shouldn't) forgotten who she was?

2. J. Periam Danton, *Book Selection and Collections: A Comparison of German and American University Libraries* (New York: Columbia University Press, 1963).

3. Ibid., pp. 69-70.

4. Frederick G. Kilgour, preface to N.S.M. Co. et al., *The Computer and the Library* (Hamden, Conn.: Archon Books, 1967).

5. Ralph E. Lapp, *The Logarithmic Century* (Englewood Cliffs, N.J.: Prentice-Hall, 1973), p. 152.

6. Howard Mumford Jones, "Modern Scholarship and the Data of Greatness," in ed. Francis Sweeney, *The Knowledge Explosion: Liberation and Limitation* (New York: Farrar, Straus, and Giroux, 1966), pp. 27-28.

7. William Morris Davis, *The Coral Reef Problem*, reprint of 1928 ed. (New York: AMS Press, 1969), p. 5.

8. U.S., National Center for Educational Statistics, *Library Statistics of Colleges and Universities: Fall 1973 Summary Data*, Part A (Washington, D.C.: Government Printing Office, 1976).

9. Carnegie Commission on Higher Education, *The More Effective Use of Resources: An Imperative for Higher Education* (New York: McGraw-Hill, 1972), p. 19.

10. Everett C. Ladd, Jr., and Seymour Martin Lipset, "When Colleges Retrench, Where Should Cutbacks Come?" *Chronicle of Higher Education* (April 12, 1976), p. 7.

11. U.S., National Center for Educational Statistics, *Digest of Education Statistics: 1975 Edition* (Washington, D.C.: Government Printing Office, 1976).

12. U.S., National Center for Educational Statistics, *Projections of Education Statistics to 1984-85* (Washington, D.C.: Government Printing Office, 1976).

13. Alfred North Whitehead, *The Aims of Education* (New York: Free Press, 1929), p. 4.

14. Ibid., p. 93.

15. Ibid., p. 101.

16. Ibid., p. 1.

17. Ibid., p. 11.

# 7  MISCELLANEA

*Research and Reality*

In the September, 1959, issue of *CRL,* Robert E. Dysinger of Bowdoin, writing on "The Research Library in the Undergraduate College," tells us that "a collection which reflects the curriculum of the institution and the interests of individual scholars and is well selected and thinned will bulk large and have far in excess of 250,000 volumes." By an interesting coincidence, *CRL* statistics for 1957-58 show that Bowdoin just happens to have had 249,564 volumes in its library at that time.

At the same time, the median figure for Group II college libraries in the same set of statistics shows 130,284 volumes. At the median rate of increase, as of 1957-58, 5,151 books per year, it would take almost a quarter-century to reach the figure Dysinger indicates as a minimum figure, 250,000 volumes.

Why is there any feeling, in this day of ready accessibility of needed volumes and pages through interlibrary loan and modern copying methods, that the undergraduate college library must try to be what it can never be? An undergraduate college library is not a research library. A research library is not an undergraduate library. *Some* research can be done in *any* undergraduate college library. Most research cannot and should not be done there.

I am not arguing against the dreams of the Dysingers. It would be nice to be able to get faculty members seriously dedicated to "adding to the sum of man's knowledge" all possible "little-used materials that are important to their work." But let's face reality.

As a specific example, I again may single out Bowdoin, which in 1957-58 spent $74.50 on its library for every student in the college. The median in the 1957-58 *CRL* statistics was $44.88. If my own college could spend as much for each of its 2,000 students as

Bowdoin does for its 774, perhaps I too would dream of expanded facilities for faculty research.

But our problem is to get a sufficient budget to build up an adequate *undergraduate* library collection. We are by no means alone in this. As William Vernon Jackson comments in "The ACRL Grants Program: A Report of Its First Four Years," also in the September, 1959, *CRL,* "the quality of library resources placed at the disposal of students in liberal arts colleges," over two-thirds expended less than $10,000 yearly for library materials. He stresses that $25,000 "seems to be a kind of ceiling on the college library's book budget at the present time."

Mind you, in between 75 and 80 percent of these libraries, Jackson says, the size of the book collection was below 100,000 volumes. In fact, only 56 percent had over 50,000 volumes. And Dysinger talks so glibly of having "far in excess of 250,000 volumes!"

I believe we are doing our colleagues a disservice when we speak in exaggerated, fanciful terms that may appeal to the ivory tower-oriented academician but certainly do not face the realities of the American undergraduate college library picture as it is today. As must all college librarians, I occasionally must endure the pressures of the research-minded faculty member and administrator who sometimes seem to forget that the undergraduate college is for the undergraduate student, not for the demanding faculty members. Such statements as appear in the Dysinger article are of no help whatsoever in such situations.

As long as we have the great majority of undergraduate college libraries so far from even approaching the basic needs of the students, let us forget about priorities for faculty research demands. Don't "let them eat cake" before we have provided bread.

### A Brief Rejoinder to Bateson

In the April, 1961, *Journal of General Education,* the distinguished British bibliographer and Oxford University professor of literature, F. W. Bateson, delivered himself of a number of obiter dicta on the subject of American libraries and librarians, based on more or less "intimate" acquaintance with, according to his own figures, 7 of the nearly 2,000 college and university libraries in this country. He gave a list of rather detailed instructions on how university libraries should be run, even down to such minutiae as exactly how to catalog and classify books, how to take care of current issues of periodicals, and how to keep track of books which are temporarily moved from regular locations. This is most helpful of the distinguished scholar. I am sure, now that he has given us his wisdom and knowledge in the field of librarianship, which he rather indecorously termed "this bastard discipline," he will not mind a few suggestions from a college librarian (perhaps equally knowledgeable on his subject) on what graduate faculty members might do to help libraries and themselves and their students, also.

First, might I suggest that scholars who call names and denigrate their professional colleagues, publicly or privately, are not likely to get the fullest measure of cooperation from these colleagues. With the best will in the world, librarians will not, despite a long and honorable tradition of unstinting service, be likely to be as helpful to the snob and the self-proclaimed scholar as to the truly learned and therefore humble college professor who works *with* and not *over* his fellow laborer in the academic vineyard.

Then, may I venture to point out to F. W. Bateson, and others of his ilk, that there is fully as much objective evidence of faculty ignorance of the needed works in their own subject fields as of librarian ignorance of the sort stated and implied in the Bateson jeremiad. All too often, faculty members (of the highest caliber, professionally speaking) show a profound and sometimes almost absolute unawareness of the materials in their own fields, extending even to a rather disconcerting ignorance of what is in their own academic libraries. This may sound very elementary, but surely any college faculty member can be expected at least to know what his own library holds in the subject area in which he, the faculty member, is supposedly an expert.

Finally, may I agree with Professor Bateson when he calls his statements "harsh words, rude words, arrogant words." The same ideas in softer, more polite, more unassuming words might possibly have been more persuasive than the type of language and argument actually presented. There is no question that there is a measure of truth and salutary advice in Bateson's article; both college and university librarians and college faculty—particularly in the field of English literature—can learn from it.

But really, Dr. B., we hardly need to have you tell us librarians the so-called facts of library procedure, which most of us might happen to know already and which are not necessarily unique and original discoveries which you have so graciously brought to our attention. Read a little "library literature" (the field of librarianship happens to be rather thoroughly analyzed and abstracted) and you will undoubtedly find that very few, if any, of your suggestions are new or untried or even deserve more than passing notice.

Whoever told Bateson that library science "can ... be learnt in a fortnight" was no more accurate than whoever led him to believe that generalizations about American college and university libraries, based on most inadequate evidence, would be valid and reliable. We American librarians are an independent and varied lot, and American libraries are equally different. Certainly, as Bateson states, "Grammarians need books, and books need libraries, and libraries need librarians." But may I add one more to this chain: grammarians need librarians, too, and are more likely to have their full aid if there is less academic condescension and contumely on the part of the grammarian.

Dr. Bateson referred to "grammarians' funerals" in his peroration. Perhaps a fitting Parthian shot for this brief rejoinder might be a quotation, which seems an appropriate selection, from Browning's "A Grammarian's Funeral":

> Learned, we found him.
> Yea, but we found him bald too—eyes like lead,
> Accents uncertain . . .

Of course, we librarians can use learned assistance, but preferably from a bright-eyed fellow scholar, whose cloak of learning is worn a bit more lightly and whose accents are more certain and more to the point. For myself, I prefer to follow the banner of a José Ortega y Gasset, who said in an address to the International Congress of Bibliographers and Librarians in Paris, in 1934: "I imagine the librarian of the future as a filter interposed between man and the torrent of books." Somehow being a "filter" offers me more of a challenge than accepting the Bateson appellation of practitioner of a "bastard discipline."

## Misquoted, Misunderstood, and Reduced to Absurdity

Your editorial entitled "The Sanctity of Book Selection," in the October 1 Lj, was interesting from several viewpoints. In the first place, you said that "a fair volume of pretentious academic flotsam" comes from university presses. Yet you saw "no great additional harm" in getting this junk "if the library saves money and time thereby!" This sounds to me very much like the familiar argument of some women that it is real economy to buy two hats, even though only one hat is needed, if there is a bargain sale on two, rather than one!

You also state that those, like me, who are stressing the professional sensibility of book selection, are in danger of setting up some kind of "sacred cow." Again, I must beg to differ, since I don't think that my arguments or LeRoy Merritt's or those of others who feel as we do should be misquoted, misunderstood, or reduced to absurdity. For myself, I tried to make clear in my article, which you solicited, on the topic of small and medium-sized college libraries and their responsibility in book buying (see *Lj*, October 1, pp. 3391-92) that, as I said, "the undiscriminating purchase of the complete output of one or more publishers will mean inevitable waste, as well as abdication of the librarian's inescapable responsibilities."

Of course, I do not expect large libraries, public or university, to waste time or money where individual book selection is obviously unnecessary. All that I am after is a recognition of the fact that the dollars we spend are the public's dollars, and we have no right to follow the *ignis fatuus* of presumed economy and actually waste money in so doing.

Rolland Stevens, also in the October issue, said that I was setting up a "straw man" and then proceeded to tell me what I meant by converting my "get-'em-all" idea, which was on getting *all of any one publisher*, into a presumed argument against libraries trying to get "every printed book, pamphlet, and journal." This, of course, I never said, and I see no point in even arguing about this.

The vice-president of the J. B. Lippincott Company stated that they hope "to refine the plan so that smaller library systems . . . [public or school] may participate in it on a modified basis." I am by no means convinced that any refinements of the Greenaway Plan can get around the basic objection which I and, I believe, many other librarians have to this notion. This is, in brief, that librarians are either librarians, or they are what Archibald MacLeish called "bellboys in the halls of culture."

I found rather interesting the fact that in the same October 1 issue, in your summary of the Silver Anniversary Conference of the University of Chicago Graduate Library School (see *News,* p. 3406, 3408), you quoted their opening speaker as saying, "The library profession should accept the responsibility of becoming qualityminded guardians of man's accumulated productivity." What *possible* quality-mindedness can there be in agreeing to accept blindly, as Ohio State University does, all "titles published by major university presses in this country and of titles published by Cambridge and Oxford"? This doesn't even have the argument of the Greenaway Plan, of having any further review by the library staff of items received. By accepting the Stevens Plan, all that happens is that we substitute the judgment of publishing house editors for that of trained librarians. This, it seems to me, is an extremely doubtful basis for building up quality libraries.

## Re: Library Research

I have read and reread "A Kaleidoscopic View of Library Research," since the arrival here of the May, 1967, issue of *WLB,* with deep appreciation for the careful thought involved in, first, the selection of appropriate individuals for this symposium, and, secondly, for the extremely useful suggestions presented by the contributors. As a member of the Advisory Committee on Library Research and Training Projects, which has the responsibility of advising the commissioner of education "on general policy" concerning projects and grants approved under part B of Title II of the Higher Education Act of 1965, I found exceedingly valuable this up-to-date, concise, and practically oriented accumulation of facts and opinions on this most important topic.

In its two meetings to date, the committee has found (and I am speaking for myself here, really, and not for the entire committee, of course) that one of the more significant problems connected with giving out money for research demonstration projects is that practicing librarians seem to be much less interested in research than they really should be. Most of the requests come from the academic side as might, I suppose, be expected; but perhaps your inspirational and informational symposium may encourage ever-widening interest by all members of our profession, who really consider themselves to be professional, in the vital matter of library research. It is obvious and almost a cliché to say that there is a vast amount of untreated hypotheses or outdated research results involved in the ongoing activities of all types of libraries today; what is needed is a bringing into focus of the major problems of librarianship and, most specifically, thorough, modern research into all the problems associated with library manpower, which is now and is likely to be the truly vital problem, in all its ramifications, for the librarianship of the 1960s and 1970s.

I remember that doyen of library researchers, Pierce Butler of the University of Chicago Graduate Library School, saying over twenty years ago, in a class I was fortunate enough to have under him, that "the worst vice of the librarian is reading." Like most of his classroom apercus, this was a gnomic and thought-packed statement which I am only now beginning to understand in its fullest sense. For what it is worth, my interpretation is that the librarian who thinks that he can face up to the issues of his profession merely by reading about them is truly an enemy of the basic philosophic principles which should guide that profession.

No matter how busy we are, there is not a one of us who should not be eager to do his or her active part in carrying out that most significant responsibility of our chosen calling, to know what we are doing and why and how best to do it. To these great purposes, your symposium has been a most constructive contribution.

## Court Ruling Called a Threat to Those with "Unconventional Ideas"

The issue of academic freedom seems to me to have been pretty well concealed in the news story carried in the April 10 issue of *The Chronicle* concerning the recent decision by the U.S. Supreme Court to back an appeals court ruling "that the University of Minnesota could deny employment to a librarian because he was an 'activist' homosexual." I think the issue is there and that it needs attention and study.

Whether or not homosexuality is a "socially repugnant concept" is not at all at issue, I feel. The issue that concerns me—and should concern all connected with higher education—is whether those with "unconventional ideas" can, since the Supreme Court decision has been made, any longer have any reasonable assurance of being hired by academic institutions from now on.

The decision by the Supreme Court approved the denial of a contract by the University of Minnesota board of regents because, said the court, "the prospective employee demands . . . the right to pursue an activist role in *implementing* his unconventional ideas concerning the societal status to be accorded homosexuals."

Now, suppose a job applicant asks to be given the right to implement "unconventional ideas concerning" such matters as abortion, pacificism, atheism, contraception, marijuana smoking, pornography, or other ideas considered "unconventional" in the United States. From now on, as I read the Supreme Court decision, must prospective employees give up their freedom of speech, of action, of expression if it includes "unconventional ideas"?

All of this deserves some serious study and consideration, in my opinion, lest we drift unheedingly into a monolithic, establishment bound atmosphere for American higher education, a situation which would be both actually and potentially much worse than our present one.

## Basting the "Livers With"

Since both Ervin Gaines and Mrs. Krug referred to my share in the drafting of the present text of the Library Bill of Rights, may I plump on the side of Mrs. Krug and Mr. Harvey in this particular controversy, since it is a fact that the word "age" was added by the members of the Intellectual Freedom Committee in discussion of the draft of the Boaz-Oboler-Gaines text, as Mrs. Krug and Mr. Harvey state (*American Libraries*, October, 1971, p. 923). Even if this were not the fact, I assure you that, speaking for myself, I am entirely in disagreement with Mr. Gaines on this matter. I do not think that whether or not our society is or is not "ready to accept the philosophy enunciated in the advisory statement" is to be considered or should be considered by librarians. This is the way librarians feel, and this is the way we should run our libraries. I have written in several places and stated publicly my opinions on the reading of young people, and I do not in any way agree with "variable obscenity" as a concept "with which we can learn to live." I see no reason for "learning to live" with what we disagree with, and I think the keynote for librarians who are really concerned with intellectual freedom should be to be leaders in the fight for the freedom of the word rather than followers and adapters and "livers with," if there is such a phrase.

In sum, if there is any question about where Eli Oboler stands on censorship, I am against it. I am against it for one year olds, two year olds, ninety year olds, and everyone in between. I am against it for people of every race, of every age, of every sex—in short, for everybody. I am a little amazed to find that Ervin Gaines, who came out in favor of having in every public library a readily available collection of pornography, now has come around to what I consider a somewhat equivocal position. I hope he sees the light; I saw that light long ago, and I think it is a light that should illuminate our thinking in the years to come. If not, we might as well forget about fighting the censor. If he hasn't got the librarians against him, who will fight for the cause?

## Faculty Status for Librarians

As always, on the first reading of an Ellsworth Mason opus, I enjoyed "A Short Happy View of Our Emulation of Faculty." Then, as nearly always seems to be the case with Mr. Mason's writings on topics which do not deal with library buildings, I went back to review the article and found it misleading, rhetorical, and, in essence, almost useless to help us in our current dilemma. The dilemma I am referring to, of course, is whether or not to fight to get or keep faculty status and rank, in the present state of the library profession and in the present state of the academic teaching profession.

I believe that Mr. Mason's facts are consistently wrong in this editorial; and his conclusions, therefore, must necessarily be wrong. In the first place, it is absolutely not true that "in any university of quality, this means no promotion above the rank of instructor without a Ph.D. degree." I challenge Mr. Mason to give me examples of even a very few institutions where this is true. Secondly, it cannot be a fact that the present crop of college teachers are "opportunists," who have very low standards of classroom performance and grading, and at the same time be true that we must compete with "high-powered academicians." What Mr. Mason seems to want us to do, as academic librarians, is to meet some kind of undocumented standards which exist only in his mind and govern the typical teaching faculty member. I have been involved with academic libraries over a period of nearly thirty years, and, although my actual experience is mostly at this medium-sized university, I think that I have been around sufficiently to be a fair judge of what has gone on and is going on in both our profession and the academic profession.

I believe that the new *Joint Statement* is a good one and, like all such statements, may well be capable of some modification as experience warrants. But it is an extremely good starting point and should help the academic librarians and the college teachers to get together on at least a modus vivendi basis for the foreseeable future.

One last point about Mr. Mason's editorial: it seems to me that to say that "the only faculty benefit denied librarians is a longer vacation" is about like saying the only things lacking in the Venus de Milo are two arms. I, for one, find it extremely distressing to have to spend approximately one-sixth of my working life at the same old grind, while my confreres, who are no more capable of handling their particular jobs than I am of handling mine, are gadding about for two months each summer and for periods between semesters, while I must keep my nose to the grindstone. I do not see that it is at all a fair salary trade that librarians be paid as miserably as most of us are in relationship to standards for teaching faculty, as a sort of recompense for not having to follow the publish-or-perish and the tenure-or-sink syndromes, as he suggests. As a matter of fact, the latter part is not true at Idaho State University and, I believe, not true in most institutions of higher learning in this country which do give faculty status and rank. Tenure rules do apply to both professional librarians and teaching faculty, generally.

Sometime, Ellsworth, I would like to have you deliver a statement without being so damned oracular and positive about it! Or do I feel that way because I have some of that tendency myself?

## VERSE

### The Pace of Reading

> The books I like,
> I swallow first;
> 'Tis thus I quench
> My early thirst.
>
> The books I loathe,
> I read in haste;
> 'Tis thus I'm purged
> Of time's great waste.
>
> The books I love,
> I reread, slowly;
> 'Tis thus I'm sure
> Of pleasure, wholly.
>
> The books I hate,
> I read but once;
> 'Tis thus I know
> I'm not a dunce!

### Sabbatical Leave

> Septennial: the seventh year at last
> When all the tensing days have coiled their spring
> To make a future brighter than the past,
> To hear—and tell—what songs the Sirens sing.
>
> Within the bonds of scholars' rules, yet free
> To do what must be done, despite the fears
> Lest all the *angst* end in fatuity;
> Now is the testing of the busy years.

*Accreditation Visit*

> We few must judge, or years to come,
> What has been done, what yet may be;
> Our task—to weight, with wise aplomb,
> The ineluctability
> That all must end, that men will fail,
> That Wisdom's bark's a ship of fools.
> And so we put upon the scale
> Some art, some skill, tradition's rules
> And hope, beyond vain hope and rue,
> The measured weights may balance all
> Of learning, truth, the old, the new,
> Lest Academe see darkness fall.
> O vain and useless quest we make—
> Of Truth? A Jade. Of Faith? A Fake!

## OBOLER DICTA

1. The significance of any unequivocal statement about librarianship as a whole by any professional librarian is usually in indirect proportion to his own evaluation of its significance.
2. Librarianship as a whole is tending to concentrate more on the means of giving library service rather than on the giving of that service.
3. The librarian of today ignores the machine; the librarian of yesterday dreaded the machine; the librarian of tomorrow may be a machine—but, unfortunately, all three types are in active performance of their duties today.
4. All public librarians know that all academic librarians are overpaid and underworked; all academic librarians are certain that school librarians have it easy and get paid incommensurately for this ease; every school librarian knows that all public librarians are possessors of sinecures. All three agree that special librarianship is a cinch. Clearly, the solution to all personnel problems in librarianship is for the ALA to merge with and become part of SLA; then, to quote Orwell, "all will be equal, but some will be more equal than others."

5. The true importance of library statistics is to enable its users to know for sure how inadequate their library is in some particular respect. Maybe if there were no official library statistics, no one would worry about inadequacy, and each one of us would instead get about doing his job as best his abilities and finances permit.

6. Before every national library conference, the impossible is expected; after every national library conference, the incredible is taken for granted. Between conferences, library leaders plan for the acceptable.

7. No library literature is worth reading, let alone rereading—except the item not yet published, especially if you wrote it.

8. If all the library schools in America were piled end to end, and an *auto-da-fé* created of their staffs, maybe those who know something about librarianship would get a chance to tell what they know to prospective librarians. But it would never work, because we forgot also to burn up the accrediting agencies!

9. There are really only two types of catalogers; the ones who fuss and those who have retired.

10. Formula for a male library administrator: 20 years of experience + 1 daily sack of tobacco + 2 old jokes to use at annual staff meetings + 1 door to lock oneself behind, consume the tobacco, and then muse on the ultimate necessity of finding more and more people to do less and less work.

11. Much as some librarians would like it to be otherwise, the world views the library as a refuge from the world and librarians as unworldly refugees from the actions and passions of our time.

12. In dealing with library trustees, bear in mind that a trusty, in penological practice, is a man with a conviction who is temporarily given a responsibility without too many shackles; on occasion, in prisons, trusties have been known to riot, pillage, and burn, when not restrained by professional penologists.

13. When a library booklist becomes too contemporary, the library patron is entitled to ask if all knowledge and worthwhile opinion began yesterday.

14. In giving birth to a library building, remember that you, the librarian, are both parents; the architect is the obstetrician you consult during the gestation period; the contractor is the delivery

room doctor; and all the taxpayers and board members are merely supernumerary grandparents. The library consultant, if any, is the out-of-town obstetrician you call in for advice, usually because you don't trust your home town man.

15. The sign *SILENCE* in any library is an admission that your library is poorly planned, your administration is a failure, and your clientele are captives in a dungeon-keep rather than participants in an educational and fundamentally entertaining enterprise.

16. Although most library associations won't admit it, their major raison d'être is that they offer at least a once-a-year opportunity for some members to get away from work.

17. There are times, in dealing with an irate patron, when it is well to remember that it may be better to admit that it is possible that that dehumanized entity, the library, may be something less than infallible than to adhere to rules which may be merely the fossilized codification of past, stupid policies.

18. No library staff association in recorded history ever disagreed fundamentally on an important library policy matter with the head librarian for very long without one of three things happening: (1) the staff association reversed itself, (2) the staff association went out of existence, or (3) the head librarian left. There *is* a rumor that in 1888, on a cold Saturday in a small public library in a small town in upstate New York, a fourth event happened: the head librarian changed *his* mind. This has not yet been substantiated.

19. The American Library Association, unlike Voltaire's famous paradoxical dictum about the Holy Roman Empire, is certainly American, deals with libraries, and is an association. But it is just as certainly international in membership and responsibilities, has always dealt with many other kinds of institutions, and is occasionally prone to acting as if it were an oligarchy.

20. There is a relatively new and heady brew now available to almost every library. Its name is federal-ade. It has restorative and health-giving qualities but tends to destroy initiative and innovation if taken without due precautions. There are even some who think the Food and Drug Administration should regulate its use somehow, especially since it has a tendency to be habit-

forming. Its addicts can easily be recognized; their pupils lose their normal conformation and are replaced by flashing dollar signs.

21. The best way to get an out-of-print book quickly and cheaply is to buy it when it's in print and hold on to it until it goes out of print.

22. If and when the library gets an unexpected large amount of money and spends it quickly just to make sure that the money is spent, that library didn't deserve to get the money in the first place. It may be old-fashioned, but a "desiderata" file of expensive sets, backfiles, or even individual volumes that are readily available and sorely needed but have been put aside because of lack of funds, is getting to be one of the most useful helps in any kind of library in this day of large gifts and even larger government grants.

23. Everyone is entitled to his most intimate treasure which nothing but maturity will make him give up: the small child has his blanket or his doll; the archaic library administrator keeps his accession books.

24. No library association of any size can go two straight years without a plea for "Let the young librarians do their share," while the veterans cling desperately to every possible vantage on the road up to heading the association.

25. Since Melvil Dewey began it all, he is a convenient whipping boy for those who prefer to damn the dead rather than to analyze thoroughly the actions and needs of the living.

26. "I'm more interested in form than content," said the young cuneiform tablet accumulator, "but I'm not going to be the first to get those new-fangled papyrus rolls."

27. There is generally a great deal more effort and ingenuity and interest currently displayed in trying out various ways of frustrating book thievery than there is in encouraging new readers and greater breadth and depth of reading.

28. Hell hath no fury like a woman librarian explaining that there should be no sex discrimination of any kind in library hiring, while at the same time she is using every device known to woman to undermine the authority or take the job away from her own supervisor or administrator (male).

29. Given a choice, most book-reviewing public librarians would rather review a "juicy" novel than a dull tome on the history of the life and adventures of creatures of the early Pleistocene; but when will some librarian frankly write in a review: "This novel is no work of art, but has several exciting bits of erotica which your clientele will drool over. I did. Buy in quantity"?

30. The ancient and honorable art of buck-passing of responsibility reaches its peak of perfection when a well-intentioned ALA project, usually costing some foundation vast amounts, falls on its visionary face. Nevertheless, without those who are willing to take the risk of exploring the unknown or experimental, librarianship will never progress, as it must if it is to survive.

31. Never read any library literature over ten years old; you're too likely to find out that what you're planning to do was already tried—and failed.

32. The Library Stock Exchange reports as its most recent quotations: AUTOMATION way above earning values, but heavily speculated in; TRADITION being sold short; DEWEY, as usual, under blistering attack by new venture stocks, but holding its own; CENSORSHIP, a sleeper, with wide, unpublicized support, even by those who claim to attack it publicly.

33. No one expects librarians to lead public opinion; it would be nice, however, if, just a little more often than at present, librarians would at least express some, and on something else besides the virtues of L.C. versus D.C., or book catalogs versus card catalogs. Isn't Hubert Humphrey really a druggist and LBJ a schoolteacher by profession?

34. The recent national decline in use of the public library is easily explicable: the more money spent on supporting the places where books are available, the less people want to read there. If our seers are correct, the only solution is to start a new circulation index using as a formula something like this:

$$\frac{\text{Library taxes}}{\text{Library users}} = \text{Library book circulation}$$

The top public library, then, will be the one which uses the most tax money to yield the least service.

35. Has anyone thought of the possibility that reading is simply

becoming a vestigial ability and being superseded by listening and looking?

36. In at least one respect, the American Library Association is comparable to a major football team. It does have to plan its national conventions in advance. We are told that the limiting factors are usually the number of hotels and the amount of exhibit display and convention room available. How about planning an ALA convention sometime on a remote island with everyone asked to bring his own pup tent and bedroll? With less emphasis on housing and advertising, maybe there would be some chance to get together and talk about library problems.

37. The greatest experts on the proper methods of library education and the ones most usually ignored are the actual practitioners of the profession. Someone, sometime, should get the happy thought that library education is simply too important for the library educators, to paraphrase a famous remark about war and generals.

## BIBLIOGRAPHY OF ELI M. OBOLER, 1939-1976

1. "It Happened Five Years Ago." In *Prose Projects: An Anthology with Exercises, for Students of Composition,* edited by Josiah L. Geist and T. M. Garrette, pp. 93-94. New York: F. S. Crofts, 1939.

2. "Men Librarians." *Library Journal* 75, 2 (January 15, 1950), pp. 66, 98.

3. "Elite and the Public Library." *Library Journal* 75, 4 (August, 1950), pp. 1283-84.

4. "Idaho State College Library, Pocatello." In *The First Library Building Plans Institute Sponsored by the ACRL Building Committee,* edited by David Jolley. Proceedings of the Meetings at Ohio State University, Columbus, Ohio, April 25-26, 1952. *ACRL Monographs,* no. 4, pp. 25-29. Chicago: Association of College and Research Libraries, 1952.

5. "Congress as Censor." *Library Journal* 77, 20 (November 15, 1952), pp. 1927-30. Portion reprinted in Daniels, Walter M., ed. *The Censorship of Books.* New York: H. W. Wilson, 1954.

6. "Librarians: Active or Passive?" *Idaho Librarian* 5, 1 (January, 1953), pp. 16-17.

7. "Library Legislation Workshop." *PNLA Quarterly* 17, 4 (July, 1953), pp. 146-48.

8. "T-Formation." *Library Journal* 78, 14 (August, 1953), pp. 1305-306.

9. "O. P. and All That." *ALA Bulletin* 47, 9 (October, 1953), pp. 433-34.

10. "Chute the Works!" *Library Journal* 79, 22 (December 15, 1954), pp. 2387-89.

11. "The Regional Legislative Committee and Cooperation." *PNLA Quarterly* 19, 2 (January, 1955), pp. 80-83.

12. "Invitation." *Idaho Librarian* 7, 2 (April, 1955), pp. 37-41.

13. "Browsing at Idaho State College Library." *Idaho Librarian* 7, 3 (July, 1955), pp. 49-50.

14. "Power and Light." *PNLA Quarterly* 20, 1 (October, 1955), pp. 7-10.

15. "Faculty-Library Cooperation." *Improving College and University Teaching* 4, 2 (Spring, 1956), pp. 38-43.

16. "President's Foreword." *PNLA Quarterly* 20, 2 (January, 1956), pp. 79-80.

17. "President's Foreword." *PNLA Quarterly* 20, 3 (April, 1956), pp. 117-18.

18. "Forty-sixth Conference." *PNLA Quarterly* 20, 4 (July, 1956), pp. 151-52.

19. "The President's Report to PNLA." *PNLA Quarterly* 21, 1 (October, 1956), pp. 33-35.

20. Ed. *College and University Library Accreditation Standards–1957. ACRL Monographs,* no. 20. Chicago: Association of College and Research Libraries, 1958.

21. "An Editor Says, 'Goodbye.'" *Idaho Librarian* 10, 2 (April, 1958), p. 3.

22. "Radiation-Fallout–A Selected List." *Library Journal* 83, 19 (November 1, 1958), pp. 3069-70.

23. "Across State and Provincial Borders: What Regional Library Associations Can Do." *Mountain-Plains Library Quarterly* 2, 4 (Winter, 1958), pp. 9-11.

24. Review of *Idaho State Library Buying List of Books for Small Idaho Libraries. PNLA Quarterly* 23, 2 (January, 1959), p. 102.

25. "The Processionary Caterpillar and NLW." *PNLA Quarterly* 23, 3 (April, 1959), pp. 154-55.

26. "Libraries of Idaho: A Ten-Year Personal Report." *Idaho Librarian* 11, 3 (July, 1959), pp. 17-21.

27. Review of Schick, F. L. *Paperbound Books in America. PNLA Quarterly* 23, 4 (July, 1959), p. 201.

28. "John W. Borden, 1916-1959." *PNLA Quarterly* 23, 4 (July, 1959), p. 188.

29. "The Wonderful World of Documentation-Automation." *PNLA Quarterly* 23, 4 (July, 1959), pp. 204-205.

30. "Religion Today—A Selected List." *Library Journal* 84, 15 (September 1, 1959), pp. 2424-30.

31. Review of Lowenthal, M. F. *Book Selection and Censorship. PNLA Quarterly* 24, 1 (October, 1959), pp. 102-103.

32. "Research and Reality." *College and Research Libraries* 21, 2 (March, 1960), pp. 184-85.

33. "Pie in the Sky: Or, Let's Dream Big Dreams!" *Idaho Librarian* 12, 2 (April, 1960), pp. 77-80.

34. "U.S. Library Periodicals: A Selected List." *Canadian Library* 17, 2 (September, 1960), pp. 77-80.

35. "Get-'Em-All Theory of Book Buying." *Library Journal* 85, 17 (October 1, 1960), pp. 3391-2.

36. "New Nations: A Selected Reading List." *Library Journal* 85, 20 (November 15, 1960), pp. 4107-10.

37. "Idaho School Libraries—If Any!" *Professional Reviewer,* Idaho State College of Education (February, 1961), pp. 1-3.

38. Review of Clapp, Jane. *College Textbooks. Library Journal* 86, 3 (February, 1961), p. 562.

39. "What the Individual Means to ALA." *ALA Bulletin* 55, 2 (February, 1961), pp. 186-87.

40. "The Pre-Fabricated Librarian." *PNLA Quarterly* 25, 3 (April, 1961), pp. 63-64.

41. "Cooperation, The 'Vitalizing Blood.'" *PNLA Quarterly* 26, 1 (October, 1961), pp. 63-64.

42. "Attitudes on Segregation: How ALA Compares with Other Professional Associations." *Library Journal* 86, 22 (December 15, 1961), pp. 4233-39.

43. "Library Statistics: Why, How, and Maybe." *Idaho Librarian* 14, 1 (January, 1962), pp. 6-8.

44. "Riches and Diversity." *PNLA Quarterly* 26, 2 (January, 1962), p. 111.

45. "Brief Rejoinder to Bateson." *Journal of General Education* 14, 1 (April, 1962), pp. 69-71.

46. "Carnovsky Revisited: Or, Library Periodicals Seven Years Later." *ALA Library Periodicals Round Table Newsletter* 9 (June, 1962), pp. 3-4.

47. "Library Patron's Bill of Rights." *Idaho Librarian* 14, 3 (July, 1962), pp. 59-62.
48. "Three and Four Letter Words." *PNLA Quarterly* 25, 4 (July, 1962), pp. 235-36.
49. "For Outstanding Leadership." *PNLA Quarterly* 27, 1 (October, 1962), pp. 75-77.
50. "Let's Prove We Mean It!" *PNLA Quarterly* 27, 2 (January, 1963), pp. 114-15.
51. "'The Forts of Folly'?" *PNLA Quarterly* 27, 2 (January, 1963), pp. 21-25.
52. "Why Is a Trustee?" *Idaho Librarian* 15, 1 (January, 1963), pp. 21-25.
53. "Shera Nonsense and Some Sense." *PNLA Quarterly* 27, 3 (April, 1963), p. 187.
54. "Education and Training of Library Workers." In *Proceedings: Western States Library Extension Conference, Sun Valley, Idaho (May 27-28, 1963)*, published 1964, pp. 55-57, 59-61.
55. "Vale MLQ!" *PNLA Quarterly* 27, 4 (July, 1963), pp. 253-54.
56. "Idaho School Librarians and Salinger's 'Catcher in the Rye': A Candid Report." *Idaho Librarian* 15, 4 (October, 1963), pp. 86-87.
57. "ALA and PNLA." *PNLA Quarterly* 28, 1 (October, 1963), pp. 86-87.
58. "The Conference I Missed." *PNLA Quarterly* 28, 1 (October, 1963), p. 87.
59. "Who Is a Librarian?" *PNLA Quarterly* 28, 2 (January, 1964), pp. 137-38.
60. Reviews of Danton, J. Periam, *Book Selection and Collections*; Sheehan, Sister Helen, *The Small College Library*; and Lyle, Guy R., *The President, the Professor, and the College Library*. *PNLA Quarterly* 28, 2 (January, 1964), pp. 139-40.
61. "The Library and ISU Alumni." *ISU Today* 5, 3-4 (Spring-Summer, 1964), pp. 4-5.
62. "The Libraries of Utopia." *Idaho Librarian* 16, 3 (July, 1964), pp. 114-16.
63. "Goodbye, Reference Librarians!" *RQ* 4, 1 (September, 1964), pp. 12-13.
64. "Librarians and Politics." *PNLA Quarterly* 29, 1 (October, 1964), p. 80.
65. "'How Far That Little Candle ...'" *PNLA Quarterly* 29, 1 (October, 1964), pp. 80-81.

66. "Prospects for PNLA." *PNLA Quarterly* 29, 1 (October, 1964), p. 81.

67. "What the New Federal Library Legislation Means for Idaho Librarians and Libraries." *Idaho Librarian* 16, 4 (October, 1964), pp. 135-37.

68. "The Accuracy of Federal Academic Library Statistics." *College and Research Libraries* 25, 6 (November, 1964), pp. 464-96.

69. "The Vital Necessity of Keeping Up with the World." *Idaho Librarian* 17, 1 (January, 1965), pp. 101-104.

70. "Livison." *PNLA Quarterly* 29, 2 (January, 1965), pp. 142-43.

71. "Why a Library Card?" *PNLA Quarterly* 29, 2 (January, 1965), p. 143.

72. "Reorganize or Die?" *PNLA Quarterly* 29, 3 (April, 1965), p. 210.

73. "Weed 'Em and Weep!" *PNLA Quarterly* 29, 3 (April, 1965), pp. 210-11.

74. "Idaho Libraries and Intellectual Freedom." *Idaho Librarian* 17, 3 (July, 1965), pp. 101-104.

75. "Where Is BCLA Going?" *PNLA Quarterly* 29, 4 (July, 1965), p. 255.

76. "A Breather?" *PNLA Quarterly* 29, 4 (July, 1965), pp. 255-56.

77. Review of Moore, Everett T. *Issues of Freedom in American Libraries. PNLA Quarterly* 29, 4 (July, 1965), pp. 263-64.

78. Review of American Library Association Intellectual Freedom Committee. *Freedom of Inquiry: Supporting the Library Bill of Rights. PNLA Quarterly* 30, 1 (October, 1965), pp. 89-90.

79. "The Education of Librarians." *PNLA Quarterly* 30, 1 (October, 1965), p. 88.

80. "Exits & Entrances." *PNLA Quarterly* 30, 2 (January, 1966), p. 143.

81. "The CLR Reports." *PNLA Quarterly* 30, 2 (January, 1966), pp. 143-44.

82. "A Constitutional Crisis in the ALA?" *ALA Bulletin* 60, 4 (April, 1966), pp. 384-86.

83. "Getting Involved." *PNLA Quarterly* 30, 3 (April, 1966), p. 212.

84. "Professional Librarians Only?" *PNLA Quarterly* 30, 3 (April, 1966), p. 212.

85. "Hallelujah, Give Us a Hand-out, and Revive Us Again!" *Idaho Librarian* 18, 2 (April, 1966), pp. 46-48.

86. Review of Journal of Library History, Philosophy and Compara-

tive Librarianship. *Drexel Library Quarterly* 2, 2 (April, 1966), pp. 284-85.

87. "Librarianship & Change." *PNLA Quarterly* 30, 4 (July, 1966), pp. 264-65.

88. Review of Kuhn, Warren B., comp. *The Julian Street Library: A Preliminary List of Titles. PNLA Quarterly* 30, 4 (July, 1966), pp. 270-72.

89. "Machines & Libraries: The Parameters of Common Sense." *Iconoclast* 1, 1 (Summer, 1966), pp. 7-13.

90. "CONLIS, ALA, You, Me—And All That." *PNLA Quarterly* 31, 1 (October, 1966), p. 108.

91. "State and Provincial Surveys." *PNLA Quarterly* 31, 1 (October, 1966), p. 109.

92. "As It Was in the Beginning." *PNLA Quarterly* 31, 2 (January, 1967), p. 165.

93. "Ideas and the State University." *School and Society* 95, 2287 (February 4, 1967), pp. 78-80. Also in Lehrer, Stanley, ed. *Leaders, Teachers, and Learners in Academe: Partners in the Education Process.* New York: Appleton-Century-Crofts, 1970.

94. Review of Shores, Louis, et al., eds. *The Library-College. Library Journal* 92, 10 (May 15, 1967), p. 1909.

95. Review of Shores, Louis. *Origins of the American College Library, 1638-1800. Journal of Library History* 2, 3 (July, 1967), pp. 253-54.

96. "Library Associations: Their History and Influence." *Drexel Library Quarterly* 3, 3 (July, 1967), pp. 255-62.

97. Review of Marshall, J. D., ed. *Library in the University. Library Journal* 92, 15 (September 1, 1967), p. 2903.

98. "Intellectual Freedom, Censorship, and Library Associations." *Drexel Library Quarterly* 3, 4 (October, 1967), pp. 399-400.

99. "Academic Library Statistics Revisited." *College and Research Libraries* 28, 6 (November, 1967), pp. 407-10.

100. "Adventures of a Library Periodical Editor." *PNLA Quarterly* 32, 2 (January, 1968), pp. 19-21.

101. "The Grand Illusion." *School Library Journal* 14, 7 (March, 1968), pp. 103-105. Also in *Library Journal* 93, 6 (March, 1968), pp. 1277-79. Also in Moon, Eric, ed. *Book Selection and Censorship.* New York: R. R. Bowker Company, 1969. Also in *Issues in Children's Book Selection.* New York: R. R. Bowker Company, 1973.

102. Review of Carlson, William H. *In a Grand and Awful Time. Library Quarterly* 38, 2 (April, 1968), pp. 189-91.

103. "What Is a Librarian? Or, Mousetraps, Beehives, and Shark Anklets." *Library School Review* (October, 1968), pp. 9-11.

104. "The New Morality and the Old Librarian." *ALA Bulletin* 62, 11 (December, 1968), pp. 1369-73.

105. Review of McLuhan, Marshall. *Understanding Media.* In *The McLuhan Explosion: A Casebook on Marshall McLuhan and Understanding Media,* edited by H. H. Crosley and G. R. Bird. New York: American Book Company, 1968.

106. "The Library Is Dead: An Irrepressibly Hopeful Elegy." *Idaho Librarian* 21, 1 (January, 1969), pp. 3-8.

107. Various book reviews in Cooley, Margaret, ed. *The Library Journal Book Review, 1967.* New York: R. R. Bowker Company, 1969.

    a. Review of Grannis, Chandler B., ed. *What Happens in Book Publishing,"* pp. 146-47.

    b. Review of Beam, Lura. *He Called Them by the Lightning,* p. 162.

    c. Review of Beggs, David W., and Buffie, Edward G., eds. *Nongraded Schools in Action: Bold New Venture,* p. 163.

    d. Review of Harbin, Calvin E. *Teaching Power,* p. 168.

    e. Review of Janowsky, Oscar I., ed. *The Education of American Jewish Teachers,* p. 169.

    f. Review of Koening, Allen E., and Bill, Duane B., eds. *The Farther Vision,* p. 170.

    g. Review of Kozol, Jonathan. *Death at an Early Age,* p. 170.

    h. Review of Winger, Nathan H. *Jewish Education in a Pluralist Society,* p. 175.

    i. Review of Murrow, Edward R. *In Search of Light,* p. 247.

    j. Review of Whitman, Ruth, ed. *An Anthology of Modern Yiddish Poetry,* p. 418.

    k. Review of Stearn, Gerald E., ed. *McLuhan: Hot & Cold,* p. 550.

    l. Review of Stember, Charles H., et al. *Jews in the Mind of America,* p. 580.

    m. Review of Lewis, Robert. *Michel, Michel,* p. 666.

108. "Copy Rights and Wrongs." *Idaho Librarian* 21, 2 (April, 1969), pp. 63-69.

109. "Hold! The Prospective ALA Dues Increase." *Library Journal* 94, 12 (June 15, 1969), pp. 2412.

110. "All or Nothing at All." *ALA Newsletter on Intellectual Freedom* 18, 4 (July, 1969), p. 70.

111. Various book reviews in Cooley, Margaret, ed. *The Library*

*Journal Book Review, 1968.* New York: R. R. Bowker Company, 1969.

a. Review of Kogos, Fred. *A Dictionary of Yiddish Slang and Idioms,* p. 22.

b. Review of Rosten, Leo. *The Joys of Yiddish,* p. 34.

c. Review of Young, W. Arthur, and McGivering, John H. *A Kipling Dictionary,* p. 44.

d. Review of Rosenthal, Raymond, ed. *McLuhan: Pro and Con,* p. 190.

e. Review of DeVera, Jose Mario. *Educational Television in Japan,* p. 195.

f. Review of Mack, Raymond W., ed. *Our Children's Burden,* p. 202.

g. Review of McLean, Roderick. *Television in Education,* p. 202.

h. Review of Spackman, Peter, and Ambrose, Lee, eds. *The Columbia University Forum Anthology,* p. 363.

i. Review of Zweig, Paul. *The Heresy of Self-Love,* p. 369.

j. Review of Zeldis, Chayym. *Seek Heaven,* p. 451.

k. Review of Kena, George F. *Democracy and the Student Left,* p. 479.

l. Review of Domhoff, G. W., and Hoyt, B. Ballard, comps. *C. Wright Mills and the Power Elite,* p. 586.

m. Review of Brassille, Keefe. *The Cannibals,* p. 675.

n. Review of Levi, Uri. *The Assassin,* p. 711.

112. "Twenty Years an Idaho Librarian." *Idaho Librarian* 21, 3 (July, 1969), pp. 95-99.

113. Review of Bevis, Dorothy. *An Inventory of Library Services and Resources of the State of Washington, 1965. PNLA Quarterly* 33, 4 (Summer, 1969), p. 33.

114. "World Disarmament: A Selected Reading List." *Choice* 6, 5-6 (July-August, 1969), pp. 630-32.

115. "The Case of ALA Regional Annual Conferences." *ALA Bulletin* 73, 8 (September, 1969), pp. 1099-101.

116. Review of Simsova, S., ed. *Nicholas Rubakin and Bibliopsychology." Journal of Library History* 4, 4 (October, 1969), pp. 355-57.

117. "The Irrelevance of Relevance." *Wilson Library Bulletin* 44, 8 (April, 1970), pp. 869-80.

118. Various book reviews in Serebnick, Judith, ed. *The Library Journal Book Review, 1969.* New York: R. R. Bowker Company, 1970.

a. Review of Skornia, Harry J., and Ritson, J. W., eds. *Problems and Controversies in Television and Radio: Basic Readings,* p. 195.

b. Review of First, Wesley, ed. *University on the Heights,* p. 200.

c. Review of Buchen, Irving H. *Isaac Bashevis Singer and the Eternal Past,* p. 338.

d. Review of Allentuck, Marcia, ed. *The Achievement of Isaac Bashevis Singer,* p. 360.

e. Review of Malin, Irving, ed. *Critical Views of Isaac Bashevis Singer,* p. 360.

f. Review of Mintz, Jerome R. *Legends of the Hasidim,* p. 417.

g. Review of Morgan, George W. *The Human Predicament,* p. 418.

h. Review of Bontemps, Arna, comp. *Hold Fast to Dreams,* p. 437.

i. Review of Howe, Irving, and Greenberg, E., eds. *A Treasury of Yiddish Poetry,* p. 444.

j. Review of Wagoner, David. *New and Selected Poems,* p. 457.

k. Review of Lewis, Jerry D., ed. *Tales of Our People,* p. 737.

l. Review of Rabikovitz, Dalia, ed. *The New Israeli Writers,* p. 752.

m. Review of Singer, Isaac Bashevis. *The Estate,* p. 762.

119. "Congress as Censor." *Library Trends* 19, 1 (July, 1970), pp. 64-73.

120. "Co-operation Among Idaho's Academic Libraries." *Bookmark* 23, 1 (September, 1970), pp. 7-8.

121. "Displays for the Academic Library." *Idaho Librarian* 22, 4 (October, 1970), pp. 135-38.

122. "The Politics of Pornography." *Library Journal* 95, 22 (December 15, 1970), pp. 135-38.

123. Various book reviews in Serebnick, Judith, ed. *The Library Journal Book Review, 1970.* New York: R. R. Bowker Company, 1971.

a. Review of *The Arts on Campus,* p. 44.

b. Review of Stein, Jean. *American Journey: The Times of Robert Kennedy,* p. 158.

c. Review of Bialik, Chayim Nahman. *Bialik Speaks,* p. 342.

d. Review of De la Mare, Walter. *Complete Poems,* p. 447.

e. Review of Ginsberg, Louis. *Morning in Spring,* p. 450.

f. Review of Lask, Thomas, ed. *The New York Times Book of Verse,* p. 456.

g. Review of Blum-Alquit, Eliezer. *Revolt of Apprentices,* p. 701.

h. Review of Glatstein, Jacob. *Homeward Bound,* p. 724.

i. Review of Orpas, Yitzhak. *The Death of Lysandra,* p. 753.

j. Review of Singer, Isaac Bashevis. *A Friend of Kafka,* p. 765.

k. Review of Yaffe, James. *The Voyage of the Franz Joseph,* p. 780.

124. "Everything You Always Wanted to Ask About Censorship (But Were Afraid to Ask) Explained." *American Libraries* 2, 2 (February, 1971), pp. 194-98.

125. "Whither Are We Drifting?" *PNLA Quarterly* 35, 2 (Winter, 1971), pp. 9-10.

126. "Sabbatical Leave" (poem). *AAUP Bulletin* 57, 3 (September, 1971), p. 376.

127. "Viewpoint: The Case Against 'Liberal' Censorship." *ALA Newsletter on Intellectual Freedom* 21, 1 (January, 1972), p. 30.

128. "Planning for a Five-Year Plan." *Idaho Librarian* 24, 2 (April, 1972), pp. 44-48.

129. "Pornography in Modern America." *Idaho State Journal* (June 2, 1972), sec. C, p. 5.

130. Various book reviews in Serebnick, Judith, ed. *The Library Journal Book Review, 1971.* New York: R. R. Bowker Company, 1972.

a. Review of *Wunnerful, Wunnerful!: The Autobiography of Lawrence Welk,* p. 143.

b. Review of Passman, Arnold. *The Dee Jays,* p. 149.

c. Review of Morris, Norman. *Television's Child,* p. 169.

d. Review of Hodgkin, R. A. *Reconnaissance on an Educational Frontier,* p. 177.

e. Review of *The Task of Universities in a Changing World,* p. 183.

f. Review of Yudkin, Michael, ed. *General Education,* p. 185.

g. Review of Howe, Irving, and Greenberg, Eliezer. *Voices From the Yiddish,* p. 300.

131. Review of Shogan, Robert. *A Question of Judgment: The Fortas Case and the Struggle for the Supreme Court. ALA Newsletter on Intellectual Freedom* (November, 1972), pp. 166-70.

132. Various book reviews in Fletcher, Janet, ed. *The Library Journal Book Review, 1972.* New York: R. R. Bowker Company, 1973.

a. Review of Messerli, Jonathan. *Horace Mann,* p. 124.
b. Review of Mason, Edwin. *Collaborative Learning,* p. 124.
c. Review of Pearl, Arthur. *The Atrocity of Education,* p. 177.
d. Review of Sowell, Thomas. *Black Education,* p. 179.
e. Review of Liptzin, Sol. *A History of Yiddish Literature,* p. 316.
f. Review of Glatstein, Jacob. *The Selected Poems of Jacob Glatstein,* p. 367.

133. "Oboler." In Wedgeworth, Robert, et al. "Social Responsibility and the Library Bill of Rights: The Berninghausen Debate." *Library Journal* 98, 1 (January 1, 1973), pp. 29-30.

134. "The Publications of the PNLA." *PNLA Quarterly* 37, 3 (Spring, 1973), pp. 17-23.

135. "Sights, Sounds, and Prints." *Idaho Librarian* 24, 3 (July, 1973), pp. 95-99.

136. "'Just Like the Child in the Family': Paternalistic Morality and Censorship." *Library Journal* 98, 15 (September 1, 1973), pp. 2395-98.

137. "Cow College Research—Who Gets the Help?" *Western Critic* 11 (December 8, 1973), pp. 3-4.

138. "Selling the Academic Library." In *Public Relations for Libraries: Essays in Communications Techniques,* edited by Allan Angoff, pp. 133-49. Westport, Conn.: Greenwood Press, 1973.

139. Various book reviews in Fletcher, Janet, ed. *The Library Journal Book Review, 1973.* New York: R. R. Bowker Company, 1974.
a. Review of Willingham, Warren W., et al. *The Source Book for Higher Education,* p. 31.
b. Review of Heller, L. G. *The Death of the American University,* p. 173.
c. Review of Dwyer, William M. *What Everyone Knew About Sex,* p. 280.
d. Review of Holtz, Avraham. *Isaac Dov Berkowitz,* p. 310.
e. Review of Miron, Dan. *A Traveler Disguised,* p. 324.
f. Review of Amichai, Yehuda. *Songs of Jerusalem and Myself,* p. 370.
g. Review of Kovner, Abba. *A Canopy in the Desert,* p. 379.
h. Review of Kahane, Meir. *Time to Go Home,* p. 529.

140. "Public Relations and Intellectual Freedom." *PNLA Quarterly* 39, 3 (Spring, 1974), pp. 17-21.

141. "Obscenity and Pornography: The Legal Question." *Idaho State Journal* (June 28, 1974), sec. C, p. 15.

142. *The Fear of the Word: Censorship and Sex.* Metuchen, N.J.: Scarecrow Press, 1974.

143. "You've Got to Be Carefully Taught." *Western Critic* (October 27, 1974), pp. 5-7.

144. "The Freedom to Choose: A Reply to 'Freedom from Filth.'" *Intellect* 103, 2362 (January, 1975), pp. 263-64.

145. "Scribe of the Wild West That Wasn't: Clarence E. Mulford." *Idaho State Journal* (March 7, 1975), sec. C, p. 5.

146. "Thoughts Concerning Censorship Disputes." *Idaho Librarian* 27, 4 (October, 1975), pp. 138-39.

147. "Accreditation Visit" (poem). *Journal of Academic Librarianship* 1, 3 (Fall, 1975), p. 19.

148. "The Free Mind: Intellectual Freedom's Perils and Prospects." *Library Journal* 101, 1 (January 1, 1976), pp. 6-9.

149. "The Building of a Story and the Story of a Building." *Idaho Librarian* 28, 1 (January, 1976), pp. 6-9.

150. Review of Bickel, Alexander. *The Morality of Consent. ALA Newsletter on Intellectual Freedom* 25, 1 (January, 1976), pp. 6-7.

151. "'The Old Man on the Hill.'" *ALA Newsletter on Intellectual Freedom* 25, 1 (January, 1976), p. 7.

152. "Alphabetitis" (poem). *American Libraries* 7, 2 (February, 1976), p. 97.

Brief Reviews:

*Library Journal* (about ten a year since 1953); *Choice: Books for College Libraries* (since magazine's beginning in March, 1964); *ALA Newsletter on Intellectual Freedom.*

Play Reviews:

*ISC and ISU Bengal,* about four reviews a year between 1950 and 1964, and one review in 1968.

Columns:

"You're Invited." Weekly in the *Intermountain* (Pocatello, Idaho), August, 1960, to February, 1965.

"It Seems to Me." Weekly in *Idaho State Journal* (Pocatello, Idaho), August, 1960, to February, 1965.

Irregular columns in *Intermountain Observer* (Boise, Idaho), September 1967, to October, 1973.

Editor:

*ALA Library Periodicals Round Table Newsletter,* 1961.

*Idaho Librarian* (quarterly publication of the Idaho Library Association), February, 1951, to October, 1954; and July, 1957, to April, 1958.

*Little Flights of Fancy,* by James D. Carey (memorial volume to ISC student newspaper columnist), 1956.

*PNLA Quarterly* (official organ of the Pacific Northwest Library Association), October, 1958, to June, 1967. Awarded *H. W. Wilson Company American Library Association Library Periodical Award,* 1964.

*Temple Topics* (monthly newsletter of Temple Emanuel, Pocatello, Idaho), 1969 to 1973.


Prepared the following Idaho State College and Idaho State University Library Reading Lists:

Reading List No. 1, *Interesting Browsing Room Books for Men* (Spring, 1958).

Reading List No. 2, *Interesting Browsing Room Books for Women* (Spring, 1958).

Reading List No. 4, *Radiation and Fallout* (September, 1958).

Reading List No. 8, *Religion and the College Student* (September, 1959).

Reading List No. 13, *The New Nations* (September, 1961).

Reading List No. 35, *The Freedom to Read* (March, 1963).

Reading List No. 39, *Poverty in the United States* (December, 1964).

Reading List No. 40, *Profiles of the Future* (March, 1965).

Reading List No. 46, *Academic Freedom and Academic Responsibility* (March, 1967).

Reading List No. 47, *Urban Renewal* (March, 1969).

Reading List No. 48, *The American University Today* (March, 1969).

Reading List No. 63, *World Disarmament* (October, 1969).

Reading List No. 67, *The End of the Empires* (February, 1970).

Reading List No. 74-1, *The Unexplained: Science, Fraud, or the Inexplicable* (1974); co-compiled by Dorothy Jacob, reference librarian. Also reprinted in *Readers Advisory Service Selected Topical Booklists,* vol. 2, no. 2, distributed by Science Associates/International (1975), pp. 109-1 to 3.

Reading List No.77, *Smoking, Alcoholism and Drug Abuse* (January, 1971); co-compiled by Margaret Linden, social science librarian).

# INDEX

## About the Author

A past president of the Idaho State Library Association, Eli M. Oboler is the university librarian at Idaho State University Library, Pocatello. He specializes in the history of intellectual freedom and censorship. Having written for such journals as the *Idaho Librarian, Library Journal, PNLA Quarterly,* the *Journal of Academic Librarianship,* and the *ALA Bulletin,* he is the author of *The Fear of the Word,* published in 1974.

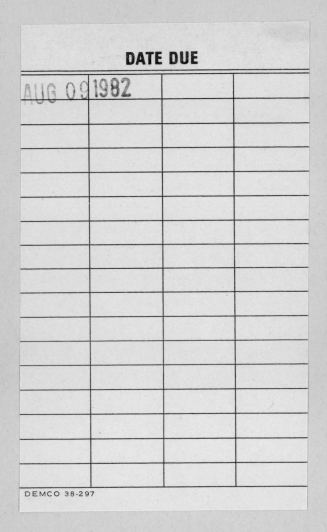

## DATE DUE

| AUG 09 1982 | | | |
|---|---|---|---|
| | | | |
| | | | |
| | | | |
| | | | |
| | | | |
| | | | |
| | | | |
| | | | |
| | | | |
| | | | |
| | | | |
| | | | |
| | | | |
| | | | |

DEMCO 38-297